Blank:
A Memoir

The Year I Felt the Humming in My DNA

PATRICIA HAVENS

Blank: A Memoir by Patricia Havens

This is a memoir, based on the author's recollections of events and conversations, personal correspondence, and journals. Some names and identifying details have been changed to protect the privacy of individuals.

ISBN: 979-8-5644488-2-6

Printed in the United States of America

Cover image by Gerd Altmann from Pixabay

First printing, 2020

*This book is dedicated to
my children, Leia, Kelsey, and Jesse*

CHAPTER ONE

Taking a shower at two o'clock in the afternoon was not my usual style. On this particular Saturday in July 2018, however, I allowed myself to spend the morning and early afternoon doing nothing—a welcome change from the stress of the past few months.

I threw on my bathrobe and stared at my reflection in the bathroom mirror. I looked tired, despite having rested all day. I shrugged and began applying my makeup, adding an extra dab of concealer to the dark shadows under my eyes.

Where were my earrings? The turquoise teardrop ones would look so good with the black sweater and slacks I planned to wear to the restaurant. I was really looking forward to the early dinner out I had planned with my girlfriends. It was the first time since my father's death two months ago that I had felt like doing something "normal."

Watching him battle dementia had been excruciating. He had always been so engaged with life, keeping busy with his job, family, and activities at the local Lions Club. After my mother's death he continued to go out to dinner and play cards with his friends—until his health began to fail. Then my days became a wearying routine of working all day at my government job and part-time caregiving for my dad, who eventually entered a nursing home.

I headed to my bedroom and began rummaging around the clutter on top of my dresser. A few pairs of earrings, but not the ones I wanted. Stray notes and scraps of paper were strewn about, and a large post-it note caught my eye. "Call Michael after Kevin takes the test," I had scribbled on the post-it. Oh, yeah. I need to follow up with my cousin Kevin. I had asked him to take a DNA test after I had been contacted by a man named Michael.

"Your name was listed on the genealogy report I recently received," Michael had told me over the phone. "I'm trying to find out how we might be related. My mother was adopted and I'm looking for her family." He had submitted a mouth swab sample to one of the biotechnology companies that provide information about DNA relatives, ancestral origins, and health markers. My name had appeared on his report because I, too, had recently submitted a sample to the same company. I had given my permission to be contacted by anyone who shared my DNA and had taken the same DNA test.

It was my son Jesse who had given me the test as a gift last Christmas. I received my results in February 2018—around the time Michael had contacted me—but I hadn't noticed anything unusual other than the fact that I was apparently a lot more "Irish" than I thought (rather than German). I had no idea why my name had appeared on Michael's report.

As the weeks went by, I had been far too busy with work and caring for my father to think too much about Michael and his dilemma. Eventually, though, I called my cousin Kevin.

"Kevin, this guy keeps getting ahold of me and wanting to find out if he's related to our family somehow. His mom was adopted. Can you take the DNA test and help us clear up the mystery?"

"I could, but my suggestion would be to just go talk to your dad," he said. "Maybe he knows something."

My father was sick and I didn't know how he might respond, but I took his advice to heart. "Okay," I said reluctantly. "I'll do that first."

I took a picture of Michael with me to the nursing home. "He says he's my cousin," I explained to my father. "We sent in DNA samples and the biotech company sent back a report that shows we're related. I thought I knew all my cousins. Do you know anything about him?"

My father had a strange look on his face, almost as if he was looking for my approval. I wasn't sure he completely understood what I was asking. "Well, your Grandpa McNeilly may have had a couple secrets in the woodpile," he said.

What did that mean? Grandpa and Grandma McNeilly had always seemed to be very much in love—almost like adolescents at times. It was hard to imagine my grandfather cheating on my grandmother.

Our visit concluded without my learning anything that I could pass on to Michael.

Not long after that visit, my father passed away. I went back to work and tried to deal with my grief while also dealing with all the practical matters that arise when a parent dies. When I saw the note on my dresser, I reminded myself that I still needed to follow up with my cousin Kevin to see if he took the DNA test.

I still hadn't found my earrings when the doorbell rang. Making sure my bathrobe was securely belted, I opened the front door. The mailman greeted me cheerfully and handed me an envelope. "Oh, thanks," I said as he turned and walked back into the sunshine. What a beautiful day to relax and laugh with my friends over a meal, I thought. It should be fun.

I looked at the return address on the envelope. It was from my cousin Kevin. Maybe he had gone ahead and taken the DNA test and decided to send me a copy of the results.

I had no idea the contents of the envelope I held in my hand would change my life forever.

CHAPTER TWO

It was not a DNA report after all, but a typewritten letter.

Hi Trish,

It is with love and support that we write to you today. We are writing with what will assuredly be shocking and potentially upsetting information.

Our hope had been that you and your dad could talk about this and together gain some peace and understanding. With the passing of your father this is no longer possible.

The truth is, you were adopted.

I nearly dropped the letter on the floor. Several thoughts raced through my mind. Was this some kind of joke? Adopted? What was Kevin talking about? And who is "we"? Oh, he must mean his sister, my other cousin Colleen.

My hands started shaking a little, but I kept reading.

It was over fifty years ago and times were much different then. We are not sure why your parents could not tell you, but we know that they raised you with all the love and care they would have ever given to the daughter that they could not have on their own.

We have been struggling with finding the right way

and time to share this with you. We had hoped to talk to you face to face when you traveled through Montana on your way home to Washington. When you first called about taking the DNA test, I tried to gently push you toward speaking with your father about this, hoping that he might feel it was the right time to reveal what he had held inside for so many years. I was concerned that if I came out and told you right away, your dad's condition could become much worse if he was confronted directly. The hope was that he would tell you on his own volition. I did not feel it was my place to say what he could not.

When I was a boy, 11 or 12 years old, my mother told me you were adopted. I'm not sure why she told me this, but she did (she also told my siblings when they were around the same age). A year or so later, while we visited your family. I inappropriately spoke up that I knew you were adopted. Things got very serious and I was told by your mother and our grandmother, in no uncertain terms, that I was never to speak of this again and you were not to find out. It was a powerful moment and I never spoke of it again. We were just kids and I never gave it much thought after that. As young adults, you and I were not particularly close and on the rare occasion that I did think about it, I certainly did not feel it was my place to tell you something that your still living parents would not. Then in February you called with news that a cousin, who you had never heard of, had contacted you. Initially I was upset with Wayne when he said this unknown cousin probably had something to do with Grandpa McNeilly. Then I thought, maybe there was something to this, maybe there was more to the story. This uncertainty and confusion led me to taking the genetics test myself. My intent was to provide you with evidence that questioned your parents' accounting, and perhaps compel your father to tell you the truth. This, of course, was not to be. Sadly, he passed away before I received my test results. I got my test results about a month ago. You are not listed in my DNA relatives.

I tried to digest all the information at once. None of the cousins or other relatives I knew had appeared on my own DNA report because they hadn't taken the test—or if they had, they hadn't given the company permission to share the results with me. So Kevin's report was the first one where my name should have appeared—except it didn't.

You are not listed, he had written.

I was not there because I had been adopted.

My legs buckled and for a moment I couldn't breathe. I grabbed the back of a nearby chair and tried to steady myself. I needed to sit down.

I stared into space, unseeing, as a thousand thoughts about my parents and my childhood swirled around my brain. I dreaded reading the rest of the letter, but I forced myself.

As you know, those were very different times and we are sure your parents had their reason for keeping this from you. We now live in very transparent times, where information is much more abundant and obtainable. We also live in a time when openness and acceptance are hopefully more easily embraced, where we don't need to hide who we are and what might have happened in the past. There is no doubt that this news is incredibly shocking and will affect the rest of your life. We hope that with time it helps your understanding of who you are and where you come from. We hope that in time you can find peace and are able to forgive your parents for not sharing this vital information with you. Undeniably they thought they were doing what was best.

We completely understand that you may be upset with us for not having told you before. We hope you can understand why we did not. We want you to know that we very much appreciate you. We are thankful that we have become closer over the past decade or more. We thought a letter might give you some time to contemplate and process this surprising information and of course we are eager to talk with you when you feel you are ready.

With sincerity and compassion, your loving cousins

I re-read the letter several times. *Our hope had been that you and your dad could talk about this.* But my father hadn't said a word about it when I visited him. Had dementia caused him to forget that I wasn't his biological daughter? Or had he been determined to keep the secret until the end?

I was fifty-eight years old, not a young woman learning about her true history early in life. I had married, had children, raised them as a single mother, had a long career—and suddenly I felt as if my entire life had been based on a lie.

I walked around my house, feeling disoriented, my mind racing. Shock gave way to grief as tears streamed down my cheeks. I couldn't even begin to process what I had just learned.

That relaxing dinner with my friends was now out of the question. My cancellation was met with astonishment at my news and words of comfort.

I stayed in my robe and tried to make sense of things; when I couldn't, I spent the next few days in deep grief.

CHAPTER THREE

Some people say when you are about to die, your whole life flashes before your eyes. When I found out I was adopted, my whole childhood flashed before my eyes.

I was about eight years old. My mother was driving, and I was sitting in the passenger seat. I pulled the visor down and spent several minutes examining my reflection in the small mirror.

"Mom, I'm looking at my nose and it isn't like yours or Daddy's at all. How come?"

"Well, I don't know who you get your nose from, but there are lots of people in our family so you must look like someone. We all started with Adam and Eve, you know."

I wasn't sure what Adam and Eve had to do with my nose. "Oh, Mom!" I said in frustration. Her answer also made me feel a little better, though. I did belong to the family, in spite of my nose.

I remembered a time when I was old enough to notice that there didn't seem to be any pictures of me as a newborn. I was folding laundry on top of the kitchen table when I mentioned this to my mother. I don't recall if I used the exact words, "Am I adopted?" but I remembered what happened next. My mother grabbed my hand and marched me into her bedroom, seemingly upset. She opened a dresser drawer and pulled out a piece of paper.

"Do you know what this is?" she asked.

I was confused. "No."

"This is your birth certificate. Look, here is my name, Bernadette, and here is Daddy's name, Wayne. We are your parents. So I don't want to hear any more about it."

Suppressed memories of childhood conversations and random incidents were continuing to resurface. The first night after I learned I was adopted, I didn't sleep at all and only fitfully the next night. It was a pattern that would continue for far longer than I could have imagined.

The day after I read Kevin's letter, I began calling my cousins. One by one they reluctantly confirmed they knew I was adopted—or at least they didn't deny knowing.

"My mother told me a long time ago that your mom couldn't have children, so she adopted you and your brother. Sorry, Trish, I don't know much more than that."

"We were told we couldn't tell you or we wouldn't be allowed to visit. It was almost like we had to take an oath of silence."

"I can't confirm anything one way or another. I just don't feel comfortable talking about it, Trish."

A sense of betrayal washed over me. How many of my "relatives" had known the truth about the circumstances of my birth but had hidden it from me for so many years? Many of the aunts and uncles who might have been able to provide more information had passed away, taking whatever they knew to the grave.

The realization that my brother had also been

adopted—years before me—was yet another shock to absorb. We had never been close and now we were no longer even in contact with each other, so I resolved to set aside any thoughts about him in order to concentrate on my own situation.

I called my son Jesse, who had given me the DNA test as a Christmas present. He almost seemed unsurprised by my news.

"It kind of makes sense, Mom," he said. "You know, I never mentioned this to you before, but whenever I'm with Dad's family, I've always noticed how they all have similar mannerisms to mine and I can feel it… this familiar energy or whatever you want to call it. Whenever I was around your mom and dad, well, I didn't feel anything at all. When I'm with my dad's family, it's like every cell in my body is vibrating and humming on the same frequency."

I considered his words. "Well, you're a scientist, after all," I said. "Maybe you're right. When we're around our biological family, we can feel a sort of humming in our DNA. Electrical impulses in our cells recognizing the same electrical impulses in other people's cells."

"Exactly," he said.

Jesse's words reinforced the feelings I'd had all my life—like I didn't belong in my family. My parents were so different from me in temperament and personality, not to mention interests and hobbies—but that happens even in biologically related families, so there had to be something else.

"You said you never felt that humming in your DNA with my parents. Well, Jesse, I don't think I ever did, either."

Jesse and I would talk at length in the weeks and months ahead. I was thankful he was not only willing to take the time to listen to me, his background in science and geophysics engineering allowed him to bring logic and order to the mental and emotional chaos I was immersed in.

I knew I needed to call Michael, the man who had unknowingly set everything in motion when my name appeared on his DNA report. I was still feeling very raw and emotional, so I couldn't help crying a little as I blurted out the news that I had just found out I was adopted. I told him that other than my children, now he was apparently the only blood relative I had in the world.

"Whoa!" he said. "I'm in my car, so let me pull over so we can talk." I waited, cell phone in hand, while he maneuvered through California traffic and parked his car.

He listened patiently to my story and told me he would do his best to figure out how we were related. He was incredibly empathetic, no doubt because his own quest had begun because his mother, Kit, had been adopted. He told me he would enlist her help in talking to other family members, many of whom also lived in California.

I took comfort from the fact that I now had someone who was willing to help me get some answers as the questions just seemed to be multiplying exponentially.

I had taken off a few days from work to deal with the shocking news I had been given, but it was time to go back to my job. Focusing on helping clients who needed assistance from the government gave my brain a brief respite from thinking about my own life, but it also meant that the limited time I had from five o'clock in the evening until the next morning was consumed by memories, questions, and trying to figure out what to do next. I slept very little and had strange, disturbing dreams every night.

By now I had shared my news with my adoptive cousins, my children, my coworkers, and my friends. One friend, who had also been adopted, informed me that in Washington state, the law regarding birth certificates of adoptees had changed. Prior to 2014, only those who were adopted after 1993 could request a copy of their original birth certificate without going through the court system. The enactment of the new law in 2014, however, meant that any adoptee who was born in Washington and was over the age of eighteen could request a copy of their original birth certificate. I immediately filled out the applicable form and mailed it in.

I kept recalling the day my mom had insisted on showing me the birth certificate that listed my father and her as my parents. "I don't want to hear any more about this," she had said. I had been so convinced that I could not possibly be adopted that I had never thought about it again.

Now I was counting the days until I could find out who my parents really were.

CHAPTER FOUR

My new relative, Mike—"No one in the family calls me Michael," he said—began sending me pictures. In turn I sent him pictures of my children. We both noticed a resemblance between two of my children and Mike's father's side of the family. This made sense since Mike's mother Kit had been adopted.

I had learned from genealogy research about something called a "haplogroup." A maternal haplogroup follows the DNA line on the mother's side—not the father's side. My son Jesse had explained that we inherit our mitochondrial DNA purely from our mothers, as they do from their mothers, and on and on through the generations.

My DNA report had shown that Mike and I shared enough DNA to be listed as cousins, but we did not share the same haplogroup. This meant that we were not connected through my birth mother. We must be related through my birth father. My birth father and Mike's birth father—that had to be the link. Unfortunately, his father had passed away, so any information had to come from others.

Mike began asking the family members on his father's side of the family about their history, and it eventually came to light that there had been adoptions within his grandmother's family. Her maiden name had been "Mahoney," so there was a chance that one of her brothers was my father. With not much to go on except a possible geographic area and approximate dates, I began searching obituaries on the internet. I was excited when I found a man whose profile looked like mine. He had my nose, the distinctive nose that my adoptive mother Bernadette could not account for.

I eagerly scanned Joseph Mahoney's obituary and noted some important details. He was Catholic, and he had planned to become a Franciscan priest. He had married several years after I was born, so it was possible that he could have fathered a child prior to that marriage. Could he have left the seminary for that reason?

A guestbook entry caught my attention. The writer was recalling all the great times her family had with Joe, his wife, and four kids. She mentioned a "favorite memory," a camping trip to ShiShi Beach, which was on the very northwestern tip of the Olympic Peninsula.

I had a picture of ShiShi Beach on the wall of my cubicle at work. I had carried that picture around for years, displaying it in every workstation because I found the rugged landscape so fascinating.

One of the other entries mentioned Joe's trips to Birch Bay every year. Birch Bay was one of my favorite places to visit. The "chill" atmosphere always had a transcendent, calming effect on me. People were known to line up on the beach to watch the most beautiful Pacific Northwest sunsets anyone could imagine. Off in the distance the San Juan Islands could be seen. My new relative Mike had mentioned his family's love of the San Juan Islands several times. I remembered a whale-watching trip I took through the islands.

So many coincidences. Were they signs?

Could this man possibly be my birth father?

I was feeling overwhelmed again by the onslaught of information I still needed to process. I decided to take a few days off from my research and just relax. The feeling of living in an alternate reality weighed heavily on me. I was troubled by the competing emotions that were fighting for ground, torn between grief over the loss of my identity and excitement about discovering my authentic roots.

I was just beginning to get my bearings again when my original birth certificate arrived.

I tore open the envelope, set the cover letter aside, and hungrily scanned the document I had been waiting for.

The mother's name was listed as Patricia Ann Miller. The father's name was not listed. And the child's name was... blank.

I was confused. My name was Patricia, the same as my mother's. Why hadn't she put that on the birth certificate? Along with confusion came a sinking feeling. Miller was such a common name. How would I ever be able to find out anything about my mother when she had such a common name?

The letter I had tossed aside provided some important information. I had indeed been born in Spokane, the same city that was listed on the birth certificate my adoptive mother Bernadette had shown me. The birthdate matched. I noted the date my adoption was finalized, about six months after my birth. No wonder there weren't any pictures of me as a newborn. I thought about how that had always bothered me. Another suspicion that had been suppressed.

My spirits were lifted a bit when I saw that they provided my birth mother's address, the residence where she had lived in Seattle. It was highly unlikely that she still lived at that address, but I had somewhere to begin my search.

I never gave a moment's thought to not looking for my birth parents. Perhaps because I discovered the truth about my adoption so late in life, I felt as if I could not afford to lose any more time. My every breath needed to be spent on finding out who I was. I could not rest otherwise.

An internet search turned up hundreds of Patricia Ann Millers. There had to be an easier way. I remembered what I had learned about "haplogroups" and studied my DNA report again. There was one individual who shared my maternal haplogroup, a man named Desmond, who was predicted to be my second cousin.

I sent him a message via the biotechnology site but heard nothing back. I sent another message, and this time he responded, *What can I help you with?*

I gave him my birth mother's name and asked if he had any relatives in the Seattle area. A flurry of messages ensued, in which I learned he did remember a cousin named Patricia, but he hadn't seen her in forty years. He was seventy years old now, he lived in California, and he was not in touch with any other family members. I was grateful when he agreed to call me the following evening.

If things turned out the way I hoped they would, this would be my first conversation with someone who actually knew my birth mother.

CHAPTER FIVE

Desmond said he would call at six o'clock, so I rushed home from work. Too nervous to eat a proper dinner, I grabbed a quick snack. I made sure I had paper and pen handy so that I could take notes. As the time drew near, I could barely contain my excitement. In one of his messages, Desmond had reiterated that he didn't want to give me any false hope or steer me in the wrong direction, but I couldn't help but feel hopeful. So far, every lead had produced an incremental amount of information. If Desmond could provide me with even one more small piece of the puzzle, I'd be grateful.

He called right on time. After a few minutes of formally introducing ourselves and a bit of small talk, Desmond gave me far more than one small piece of the puzzle. It turned out that he had actually known my mother.

"She went by the name of Patsy," he said. "She was my mother's cousin, and they were very close."

My heart was pounding so hard I could barely breathe. "You remember her? Is she alive? Do you know?"

He said the last time he had seen her was in California, where he lived, but she wasn't in very good health then. She was married and had two children, a boy and a girl.

"I don't know what happened to her after that visit," he said. "Like I told you in my messages, I really haven't seen any of my cousins in, well, at least thirty years."

"Oh," I said. "Do you know her married name? Or her children's names?"

"No, sorry. I wish I could tell you more. You know, when she used to visit my mother, I remember that she was always so kind to my sister. My sister had some disabilities, and her face would just light up whenever Patsy came into the room. So your mother was a very kind person. I have some pictures I can send to you. Oh, I can also send you a copy of my mother's marriage certificate, because Patsy's mom was a witness at the wedding."

He recalled that Patsy's mother Mary had remarried after her husband's death. Her new marriage produced three boys—Patsy's half-brothers—who might still be living in the Seattle area. One of the brothers had married into a well-respected family that owned a large department store. He gave me the brothers' names.

At the end of the conversation, he remarked, "You know, your voice is a lot like your mother's." It was one of the nicest things he could have said to me and I treasured the compliment. We agreed we'd stay in touch.

My search for my birth parents had not yet led me to them, but I had received so much comfort from my two new blood relatives—Mike and Desmond—that I knew my decision to embark on this search had been the right one.

The next step was to try to contact one of my mother's half-brothers in Seattle. By now I was becoming quite the sleuth, adept at searching the internet and social media. I found a business phone number for one of the family members and immediately called the number, not giving myself a chance to chicken out. I left a voice mail message explaining who I was and that I was trying to locate my birth mother's brothers.

When he called me back, the man I thought might be a cousin was reluctant to give me any information. Instead, he asked me a lot of questions. Finally, he said, "If we want to have any contact with you, someone will call you in the next few days." His tone was rather abrupt.

On the one hand, I could understand his reticence. He probably wanted to make sure I wasn't a scammer or a con artist. On the other hand, I knew I was a good person, and I was crushed. What if this proved to be the end of my search for Patsy?

I didn't receive a return call in a few days. To my delight, it took only a few hours. The person who called me back was my mother's half-brother Sean, who was now seventy-six years old.

My most important question was answered first. He confirmed that my mother Patsy was no longer alive.

What I felt couldn't be described as grief; that would come later. Rather, I felt disappointment, which I pushed aside in order to focus on gathering as much information as I could. Who knew if this might be my only chance to do so?

Sean told me she had died in California a few years after Desmond's last visit with her.

My existence had not been a secret. The family knew my mother had given me up for adoption. In fact, early in our phone conversation, I heard Sean say to his wife Bev, who was standing nearby, "We found her, we found her!"

I interrupted with a laugh. "I believe it was *I* who found *you!*"

We talked for two hours. My newfound uncle Sean turned out to be a wealth of information concerning my birth mother. As he described their childhood and their relationship, I scribbled notes furiously while trying not to let the fact that my mother was no longer alive take over my thoughts.

Finally, Sean confessed that he needed to go to bed. I had been so caught up in his narrative that I hadn't noticed the time. It was getting quite late. We arranged to chat again in a few days and I reluctantly ended the call. I still had so many questions.

But I had plenty to think about in the meantime. I chose to focus not on my disappointment and the stirrings of grief but on my joy about what I had learned, a litany of amazing facts and personal revelations about the woman who had given me birth.

I would never know her in this lifetime, but I was already incredibly proud of the person she had been.

CHAPTER SIX

If it weren't for the evils of gambling, my mother Patsy might have had an entirely different life.

Her mother, Mary, was born and raised in Canada. Her father, Joseph Higgins, was a prosperous businessman whose assets included ownership of a popular confectionary in Vancouver, British Columbia. Mary was an extremely attractive young woman who was sought after by quite a few wealthy young men. She was invited to parties at the finest hotels and rode around in expensive cars. My uncle Sean called it a "carefree season" for my grandmother.

Ultimately, Mary didn't fall in love with any of her high-society suitors. Instead, she fell for a gambler named Leroy Miller. Leroy, my maternal grandfather, made a good living playing cards—until the day he won a huge pot of money and was murdered by one of his fellow gamblers.

Mary was pregnant with my mother Patsy at the time of her husband's death. The scandal forced Mary's father to make the decision to leave Canada and move the family to Seattle, Washington, where he opened a café. Patsy was born soon after they arrived. As a widow and young mother, Mary was no longer being sought after by any wealthy young men. In fact, she was considered to be an "illegal immigrant" in the United States. To support herself and her young daughter, she took a job with the phone company.

The Great Depression was sweeping the country. Even Mary's father, the wealthy businessman, had to take whatever jobs he could find—including bartender and trolley conductor—when his café failed.

Prohibition was still in effect, but Mary was still a party girl at heart and Seattle had hundreds, if not thousands, of illegal speakeasies. In one of these speakeasies, she met a man named Lee Eberhardt. Lee's wife was terminally ill, and after she died Lee and Mary married—the second marriage for both. Lee's two daughters and Mary's daughter Patsy eventually became big sisters to three boys, including my newly discovered Uncle Sean.

Lee Eberhardt had been a successful businessman. He founded the Great Northern Power Company, which was Seattle's power company until the construction of the Hoover Dam put it out of business. Lee also owned a brokerage house, but he lost everything in the Depression, including his business partner, who was so distraught he jumped out of a Fifth Avenue high-rise building.

Lee turned to Mary to help him rebuild his life and claw his way out of the Depression. Just as Lee found success with a new business, General Tire, World War II commenced and rubber was commandeered for the war effort. All tires had to be retreaded. Lee Eberhardt went bankrupt.

Eventually he went to work for the Boeing Company, and the Eberhardts found stability. My mother Patsy spent a happy childhood in Seattle with her two older stepsisters and three younger half-brothers.

"I adored her," my uncle Sean had told me during our initial phone conversation. He said Patsy was like a mother to him. She knew how to create joy out of the most mundane activities. She loved to dance and taught Sean how to dance so the chore of washing dishes wouldn't be so boring. I tried to imagine them dancing around the kitchen, waving plates and bowls in the air.

To earn extra income, the Eberhardts rented out rooms to boarders. Sean recalled a house that was always filled with people—usually families with children. Patsy loved to stage plays and musicals in the back yard. She fashioned a stage curtain by attaching a sheet to a clothesline and she recruited the neighbor kids to play different parts. Pets were often coaxed into being part of a "circus."

"She had such a wonderful imagination," my uncle said. "She tried to think of different ways to teach me things. Sometimes she'd flat out make things up, like the time she convinced me the iron would explode if I touched it. She was so worried I might touch a hot iron and hurt myself."

Patsy was a straight-A student, especially advanced in her knowledge of math and science. She was so bright, in fact, that the nuns and priests at her Catholic school took notice. And they weren't the only ones. The United States military took notice, too.

I listened, fascinated, as Uncle Sean told me how the military had worked hand in hand with the Catholic Church to identify young people with high IQs, and how Patsy's high IQ had been documented at a very young age. She was still a teenager when priests, acting as intermediaries, began visiting the Eberhardt house and presenting complicated scientific problems for Patsy to solve. In return, her family did not have to pay the tuition for her education at Holy Names Academy, a prestigious private Catholic high school.

While Sean talked, I scribbled page after page of notes about my mother, trying to comprehend in a detached manner what her life had been like. At the same time, however, I was remembering my own childhood and thinking about how I, too, had staged plays in the back yard for my neighbors. How I, too, had loved to dance. How I had been an excellent student (albeit not a genius). And how I, like my mother, had been creative—a trait that was not encouraged in a family that valued practicality.

"Well, you have quite an imagination," my adoptive father said when I read one of my poems to him. "But that's not going to earn you any money." My poetry had been published in my school paper and praised by my teachers, but I listened to him and set creative writing aside. When I eventually enrolled in college (as an adult), I opted to pursue a business degree. I felt a surge of validation when Sean told me how creative Patsy had been.

My uncle said that when Patsy finished school, she was steered into a civil service career by the church. She received a top-secret clearance from the government and worked on various military installations, including one near Burns, Oregon.

By the time she headed to Oregon, she had given birth to me and decided I would have a better life with Bernadette and Wayne, who were supplied with a new birth certificate listing their names as my parents. She asked Bernadette to give me her own name—Patricia.

"She loved you very much," my uncle Sean told me.

Based on what I was learning, it seemed as though I

had quite a few things in common with my birth mother. As young women, however, our lives had taken very different turns. I spent my twenties living a fairly ordinary life as a wife and working mom in the Washington state capital, while Patsy spent her twenties working for the military.

Her most significant assignment was undoubtedly the one that sent her to the barren landscape of eastern Oregon, where she helped support an ambitious military project called "SAGE."

CHAPTER SEVEN

Harney County is the largest county in Oregon, covering about ten thousand square miles; and it's also the most sparsely populated, with fewer than ten thousand residents. Over the years Harney County's semi-arid, high-desert climate has supported industries such as logging and cattle ranching. The Burns Paiute reservation, owned by the Burns Paiute Tribe, covers nearly eight hundred acres north of the county seat of Burns.

About five miles southwest of Burns, in the middle of nowhere, one concrete block building is all that remains of the Burns Air Force General Surveillance Radar Station—the military installation where my mother Patsy worked in the 1960s. At that time it was one of forty-four mobile radar stations that supported the radar network established during the Cold War for air defense of the United States. The Semi-Automatic Ground Environment ("SAGE") system of computers made it possible to track incoming enemy aircraft and deploy U.S. planes to intercept any such aircraft.

No females were allowed on the premises of the radar station. Except for my mother Patsy.

Since she had received a top-secret clearance to work

for the military, Patsy usually didn't say too much about what she did during her time at the station, but she did share one incident with her family. It occurred during the time when the military was transitioning from ground radar tracking to using satellites. The challenge was how to keep the battery on the satellite from overheating.

"It's cold in space," Patsy said to the five engineers who were working on the issue. "Why not put the battery on the outside of the satellite where it can be cooled?"

The battery was successfully relocated.

While working at the Burns radar station, Patsy met the man who would become her husband, an officer who also worked on satellites. After the marriage, they moved to California and she gave up her civil service career to become a full-time wife and mother.

My uncle Sean had given me the name of her son, my half-brother Mark. Sean hadn't been in touch with Mark in a long time, but I found him easily through social media. He was living in Arizona.

He was surprised but not shocked by my call. I learned his sister was also living in Arizona, and that Patsy had told them both about me when they were children. He and his sister had discussed trying to find me one day, but life had gotten in the way and they had never followed through on the idea.

"We had a great childhood," he said. "We never wanted for anything. My dad worked on all these top-secret projects, and my mom helped him a lot behind the scenes. She was so smart. You know that old TV show, *Doogie Howser?* The kid who was in medical school by age eleven or so? That's how I think of our mother."

Mark was an interesting storyteller. Patsy and her husband had been good parents, he said. He had fond memories of backyard parties centered around their large swimming pool. His friends all loved Patsy, who made them feel comfortable and was a great listener. When I spoke with Mark's sister—my new half-sister—she described Patsy as a "pearls-and-white-gloves" kind of mother.

I pictured the ideal upper-middle-class American family of the 1960s.

After their children grew up, Patsy and her husband drifted apart. She wanted her independence, but she wasn't in the best of health. About six months after the marriage ended, she died unexpectedly from a blood clot in her lung.

Even though Sean had told me of my mother's death in our first conversation, I felt a stab of pain when Mark told me how she died—maybe because I was feeling closer to her by the time I spoke to Mark. I realized she was about the same age as I was now. By all rights she should have lived another twenty or thirty years. Mark said he was living with her at the time, and I was glad she had not died alone.

Once again, I felt conflicting emotions. I couldn't help but feel deep regret and sorrow that I hadn't had a chance to know her or be part of her life, coupled with the grief any daughter would have upon learning about her mother's final days. At the same time, the discovery of relatives who could paint a picture of my birth mother's personality, character, and her day-to-day life filled me with exhilaration.

An emptiness that I didn't even know existed was beginning to be filled.

After our first phone conversation, my uncle Sean had sent me a picture of my mother. She was sitting in a chair, giving the photographer a relaxed, warm smile. She was beautiful, with short, thick hair like mine—only darker. Her hair was perfectly coiffed and she wore a tasteful, long-sleeved blue dress. In one hand she held a cigarette, and I realized that like so many homemakers in the 1960s, she had probably been unaware of the dangers of smoking.

She didn't appear to be overweight, but I was glad to see that she had a larger frame, like mine. I had never been able to reconcile the difference between the petite body of my adoptive mother, Bernadette, and my own larger frame. A recollection came to mind of my mother's frustration that I was unable to fit into her own wedding dress, which she wanted me to wear when I married at age nineteen. "I know there's another dress of mine you can wear," she had insisted. How much time had I wasted as a child wondering why I wasn't as small as my mother? Now I had the answer, and it brought me comfort.

My uncle Sean was arranging for me to meet all the Eberhardts in person. They lived within a few hours' drive, so I would not need to travel too far. Two of my three children, Jesse and Leia, were planning to join me.

"Just let me know the date," my half-brother Mark said. "I'll drive up to Seattle." He hadn't seen his mother's family in many years and was looking forward to reconnecting.

"I'm excited but anxious," I told my son Jesse on the phone.

"Do you think we'll feel the humming in our DNA?" he asked. "I wonder if the electrical impulses in our biological relatives' cells will activate the electrical impulses in our cells?"

"I hope so," I said. "I guess we'll find out in a few weeks!"

CHAPTER EIGHT

Sean's daughter Kim had generously offered to host the Eberhardt gathering in her large home overlooking Lake Washington.

I wasn't familiar with the area, but when we stood on her deck and it was pointed out that one of her neighbors was Microsoft founder Bill Gates, I realized I had found myself in one of the most upscale neighborhoods in the greater Seattle area.

Despite that fact, it quickly became apparent that the Eberhardts were a down-to-earth clan that placed more value on people than things. As I interacted with them, the word that kept springing to mind was "kind." I also concluded that a family that proudly kept chickens in the back yard was probably not very pretentious.

Mark, my children, and I had arrived the previous night. Kim insisted I stay in the master suite, while the others stayed in guest or children's rooms.

I was glad we had a chance to ease into meeting all Patsy's relatives. Sean, who lived on a small island west of Seattle, offered to pick up my daughter and me before Jesse arrived from Colorado. Instead of the limousine he mentioned on the phone, he drove his large black SUV. My daughter hopped inside, but I needed a step stool to climb into the vehicle. I chuckled when I saw my son Jesse emerge from the airport. Originally, he had been told he'd be picked up in a limousine, so he wore the expression of a confident movie star as he glanced around for his limo.

"Over here, Jesse!" I called out as I noticed his slightly disappointed look.

Sean's wife Bev had accompanied him, and soon they had us all laughing and feeling more relaxed. I was glad to see that Sean was a big man. I hoped larger body types were the norm in Patsy's family. Anything that would connect me to my birth relatives was important to me.

Sean's daughter Kim—my first cousin—greeted us with a friendly smile and helped us get settled. Sean had picked up some steaks and crab for dinner, but before the meal, he said, "Now, look. We can either treat you like our guests or we can treat you like family. And if you're family, well, then you need to help out."

I was proud of my kids, who immediately jumped up and set to work. Jesse cooked the steaks, and as we enjoyed our dinner, Sean regaled us with stories about his career as a money manager. He had been an integral part of the success of the well-regarded Delancey Project in San Francisco, a program that has served as a model for helping those in recovery by providing them with a place to live and develop job skills in order to avoid homelessness.

I glanced at my children and saw they were hanging on Sean's every word, especially my daughter, who has been working with homeless populations for years.

Sean volunteered that he had been known as "the dance king of Seattle." I was tempted to share that I had won a few dance contests myself as a teenager, but I held my tongue.

When I saw Sean for the first time, earlier in the day, I felt an immediate sense of familiarity. There was just something about his eyes and his manner that resonated with me. It was as if I had known him for a very long time.

It was the same with Mark, my half-brother. He greeted me with a hug. He was a big man, too, but I didn't see much resemblance between us. That was okay, though. The conversations we'd had on the phone had been so easy, so familiar, that I had accepted him right away as my brother.

My new cousin Kim radiated positivity. She had a strong faith in God. "No family is perfect," she said, "including ours." She had been very close to Patsy's mother, our grandmother Mary, who had died in the late 1980s. At her funeral, a poem Mary had written was given to mourners.

A Mother's Reflection

And she said, "I have reached the end of my journey
and I know that the end is better than the beginning,
but my children can walk alone and their children
with them!"
And the children said,
"You will always be with us, even when you have
gone through the gates!"
And they stood and watched her as she went on,
and the gates closed after her.
And they said,
"We cannot see her, but her memories will guide us
forever."

Kim kept her copy of the poem in a photo album filled with memories of Mary's life.

In my late twenties I had a dream that put me on a trajectory of studying the tree as a symbol in many religions, especially the Bible. So I was surprised and delighted when my uncle Sean began speaking about the "Tree of Life" at dinner. I had never heard anyone else be so attuned with the tree as a symbol. I felt an unexpected spiritual connection.

To add to this feeling, a sunbeam shone through the clouds and bathed the deck off the dining room in light. God is gracing us with His presence, I thought, and I excused myself to take a picture. Soon the others followed, and we ended up taking family photos, chatting and laughing out on the deck.

More members of the Eberhardt family were scheduled to join us the next day. As we all headed to bed, I whispered to Jesse, "Well, I'm not sure if my DNA is humming yet, but I'm feeling pretty good about this visit so far."

I was surprised by how well I slept that night.

CHAPTER NINE

The backyard chickens had produced enough fresh eggs to feed everyone who was expected at Kim's house for breakfast. I was pleased my children were again pitching in, helping to fry the bacon and make the toast.

My birth mother Patsy had three half-brothers, and I had met only one: Sean. The other two, Rick and Lee, arrived for breakfast with their wives and children. Introductions were made and before long everyone was sitting down at the big kitchen table.

"I want to sit right here," my uncle Rick said as he pulled out the chair next to me.

Sean stood up and announced he had written a poem.

"My precious sister Patsy, although she's passed away,

has sent forward her little baby Tricia, within our hearts she will always stay.

We love her and her children, and celebrate their time with us,

and we look forward to many, many greetings and meetings.

Welcome to our family."

Everyone clapped, and in the pause that followed, Rick said, "Okay, try that again. That was fascinating." Peals of laughter followed, and I could see that gentle teasing was a family trait.

Rick told me a few stories about my mother. "When we were kids, my bedroom was across the hall from hers and I could see a light coming from her room at night," he said. "She loved reading and she'd crawl into her closet at night and read while everyone was sleeping."

Someone told a joke and I laughed. Rick looked at me, a startled look on his face. "You laugh exactly like Patsy!" he said. "You know how when you start to laugh and nothing comes out? She did that, too." All my life I had been kidded about my distinctive laugh. Now I knew where it came from.

He told me he had written a book and a screenplay, and once again I marveled at the creativity of my mother's family. My half-sister in Arizona had told me our mother loved to write, especially poetry.

Lee shared the story about the family's trip to County Cork, Ireland, where their ancestors had originated. "We wanted to see people who looked like us," he said. "So we walked into a pub and there was a guy who looked exactly like me. Everyone turned around and walked right back out."

I wasn't sure I got the joke, but the brothers laughed heartily. It warmed my heart to see such closeness between siblings.

The women seemed to possess a quiet strength. "We're all pretty conservative," one of my new aunts told me. "Even when we tried to go out as a group one evening, we ended up coming home earlier than the men." The rest of the women laughed.

My half-brother Mark pointed out that Patsy could

hold her own with her brothers.

"Your mother was the smartest, most intelligent woman I ever met," said Rick's wife Sue. She had come from a family that built a successful retail chain and had traveled the world, so I considered that to be quite a compliment to my mother.

I was struck by the respect the younger family members paid to the older men and women. There were no undercurrents of discord, as is the case with many families. They all seemed to be genuinely decent people who cared for one another.

At one point I teased Sean's son. "So do you remember my first phone call?" I asked. "When you told me someone would contact me if they wanted anything to do with me?"

"Is this a better welcome?" he responded with a warm smile as he gave me a hug.

I did feel welcome—by everyone. As I basked in the glow of belonging, I realized that I was indeed feeling the "humming in my DNA."

It was hard for us to leave, but my daughter had to go to work the next day. My half-brother Mark was particularly reluctant to have his time with the Eberhardts come to an end, as he was enjoying connecting with them after so many years. When Sean invited him to stay one more night at his house, his nephew eagerly accepted.

"I hate to see you go," Mark said to me. "This has been so great."

"There will be other chances for us to visit," I told him, but at that point I wasn't really sure. Perhaps this was going to be my last opportunity to talk in depth with my mother's family. I certainly didn't want to put anyone on the spot by asking if we'd meet again, so I tried to quell the hint of anxiety that was creeping into my mind.

As we headed home to Olympia, at first the car was filled with chatter as my children and I shared our impressions of our new relatives and what we'd learned from them. Soon, however, our overwhelming emotions caught up with us and we fell silent. We all knew we had to get back to our "normal" lives, which suddenly seemed so foreign. I stared out the window and listened to music as it filled the car.

I had plenty to think about, because the day had not only given me a deeper understanding of my mother's life, it had also provided me with another key piece of the puzzle surrounding my birth.

Earlier in the day I had shown my uncle Sean a photograph, and he pointed to one of the men dressed in black suits for the formal family picture.

"That's your father," he said.

CHAPTER TEN

The first blood relative I had spoken to after learning I was adopted was my second cousin Mike. He had put me on the path of researching the Mahoney brothers, his grandmother's siblings.

I had been excited to learn about a man named Joe Mahoney, whose obituary featured a profile picture. Joe clearly had my nose (or I suppose I had his nose, since he had it first). His background had raised enough questions that I was able to imagine how it might be possible for him to be my father.

I was wrong. The man my uncle Sean pointed to in the family photograph was not Joe Mahoney.

It was his brother, Tom.

The resemblance was notable. Since it wasn't a profile picture, it wasn't easy to discern if his nose was exactly the same as mine, but it was close enough for me to feel confident.

After reading Joe Mahoney's obituary, I had contacted one of his daughters, a lovely woman named Maria. She spent two hours on the phone with me, listening to my story. She was open to considering the possibility we might be related and said she would try to help me—even volunteering to take a DNA test herself. Later she sent me the black-and-white Mahoney family photo that I showed to my uncle Sean at the Eberhardt gathering.

When I let her know Sean had identified her uncle as my birth father, she told me that made sense. Her DNA results, coupled with those of her sister, strongly suggested we were cousins rather than sisters.

"So your uncle Sean knew Tom?" she asked.

"He said he recognized him because he saw him a few times at my birth mother's home," I said.

"Well, I don't think anyone in the Mahoney family knew about you," she said. "We never met your mother Patsy. Uncle Tom never married and never had any children that we knew about. But he was known for being great with kids. You should talk to one of the cousins who was close to him. I'll give him your contact information."

Maria offered to arrange a family gathering. I had just met my birth mother's family and now faced the prospect of meeting my birth father's relatives.

"I'm feeling kind of overwhelmed again," I told my son Jesse during one of our frequent phone conversations. "It's only been a few months since your Grandpa Wayne died and I've discovered I was adopted, learned that none of the relatives I grew up with were actually related to me, I have gotten copies of not one but two birth certificates, I've tracked down both my birth mother and birth father's families, and I have two new siblings! I'm exhausted. It's hard to go to work every day when I'm thinking about this all the time."

"Hang in there," Jesse said. "We're all trying to adjust. It'll just take time."

I had been contacted by the biotechnology company that performed the genetic testing. Did I want to share my story? I agreed to a phone conversation with one of their representatives and told her everything that had transpired since I had initially submitted my DNA sample. When I described how meeting my half-brother had allowed him to reconnect with our mother's family, the woman spoke about something called, "the ripple effect." This happens frequently, she said. One person finding out about their ancestry can have an unexpected impact on many other family members' lives.

It soon became apparent that "the ripple effect" extended even to the neighborhood in which I spent much of my childhood. My father Wayne was in the military, and he was transferred from California to Washington state when I was in the first grade. My parents bought a house in a family-friendly area, and the friendships I formed as a child continued unabated until adulthood. Even then, most of us kept in touch, no matter where we happened to be living.

As soon as I shared my news with one old friend, it swept like wildfire through our old circle, and friends from as far away as Hawaii to as close as across town began calling me.

"*Trish!* What the f***? You were *adopted*?" One of my friends who had stayed in the local area insisted we go to lunch. I shared my story again, and for two hours we relived our childhoods, examining them through the new magnifying glass of truth. Neighborly interactions were recalled and reassessed. Childhood conversations took on new meaning.

Another friend shared my tale with her father. "We should have been able to figure it out," he said to his daughter.

A neighbor family who had joined us frequently to go berry picking and clam digging confessed that they used to wonder how my brother and I could possibly be related, as there was no similarity in our looks, personalities, or mannerisms.

I realized that coming to terms with what I had learned was going to be a much longer process than I had imagined. I couldn't fully explain to anyone that it was so much more than just collecting interesting facts about my birth parents.

Every single thing about my life had to be reexamined.

But I could not do it all at once. I had to take one step at a time, and there were still more facts to be collected.

I accepted Maria's offer to contact the cousin who had been close to my birth father. I hoped his memories would be happy ones.

CHAPTER ELEVEN

My birth father Tom had served in the military before he met my mother. He was keenly interested in aviation, but problems with his eyesight precluded him from becoming a pilot. He was a talented photographer and after leaving the military, he worked in a photography studio for a while before becoming the primary caregiver for his mother. His love of flying and airplanes remained a constant throughout his life.

The circumstances surrounding how he met Patsy were a mystery, and my mother's relatives could tell me little about him. Uncle Sean had reported seeing him a few times at my mother's Seattle home.

I looked forward with anticipation to learning whatever Tom's family members could tell me about him.

"I have many great memories of Tom. I really do credit him for my love of exploration and wanderlust. To me, Tom was the family 'Jack Kerouac.' Every day there was somewhere to go and someone to see…"

My new cousin Tim had sent Maria a letter with some of his thoughts about my birth father. He recounted years spent hanging out with my father in Seattle. His detailed recollections painted such a vivid picture of their activities and surroundings that I felt compelled to try to recreate for myself what "a day in Tom's life" might have been like.

On my next day off, I drove to Seattle.

"When I was a kid, I spent one weekend a month with Grandma, who lived on Capitol Hill. That pretty much meant I'd hang out with Tom all day and then end up having dinner with Grandma and watching Lawrence Welk while Tom endlessly showed us photos of cousins, family outings, or various people he'd met.

"Tom took care of Grandma and the garden. He was very proud of his roses and lush green lawn. He also helped Uncle Paul, who had vision problems."

I had managed to locate my grandmother's house, situated in a quiet neighborhood of attractive homes. The houses had a lot of character, each one different from the rest. I stood in front of my grandmother's house and tried to absorb the feeling of the place. I wondered if my father had planted any of the shrubbery or plants in the yard.

My birth mother Patsy's school, Holy Names Academy, was nearby, so I took some pictures. I gazed at the windows and tried to imagine her sitting at a desk in class and staring out one of those windows. Maybe she grew bored with the curriculum, which was probably beneath her intellectual level, and daydreamed. It was interesting that she had gone to school in the same neighborhood where my father lived, but it seemed unlikely that their paths would have crossed at that time.

My cousin Tim's letter continued to recount the lazy days spent with Tom.

"Tom and I would walk to Volunteer Park, where he'd show me the fish ponds and the greenhouse. We'd walk through the rose gardens and up to the top of the water tower. There was a great view of Seattle from there. Then he'd take me to the corner store and buy me ice cream. We'd walk back up the hill to Grandma's and he'd always stop and chat with the neighbors if they were outside."

Sitting on a bench in front of the Conservancy, the historic Victorian greenhouse at Volunteer Park, I could see many of the colorful flowers through the windows but decided not to go inside. I could understand why my father walked to this park so often. I imagined it inspired his dedication to his roses and his own lush, green lawn.

I could see the Space Needle through the iconic Black Sun sculpture, which looked like an elegant black granite tire. As I wondered if Tom ever sat on the same bench, the sun suddenly shone through the clouds, just as it did at my cousin Kim's house. God was gracing me with His presence again.

"On Sundays, we'd all pile into one of the old clunker cars and drive at just about the slowest possible speed one can drive a car without getting passed by people walking. St. Joe's Church was four blocks away and it took us fifteen minutes. No traffic. Just us, slow-rolling it all the way there. You could really take everything in at those speeds. I will never forget those drives to church!

"After church, Tom would take us for a drive somewhere. The University of Washington arboretum,

Alki Beach, the Ballard Locks, Golden Gardens, Lake Washington... we'd have lunch at Spud's or Ivar's or some coffee shop. It was just so "chill" – soaking up the day, not trying to get anywhere or do anything in particular. That was Tom's pace, generally, as I recall."

Reading Tim's letter, I was a sponge, soaking up every detail about my birth father. I was beginning to form a picture of an affable fellow who was definitely not a "Type A" personality. Someone who made time for others and cultivated beauty. A son who made sure the needs of his mother and sight-impaired brother were met.

After my grandmother died, Tom stayed on in the house to take care of his brother. Tim recalled more adventures as he grew up. Betting on horses at the Longacres Race Track, watching the Blue Angels fly over Puget Sound, taking the ferry to see the Navy fleets in Bremerton. *"Most everywhere we'd go, he'd know someone. The waitress, some guy at the golf course. He'd tell them meandering stories about where we'd been. And he always, always, had photos to show. For me he exuded Seattle. He loved that place."*

He always had a camera in his hand. Maria told me the family always teased him about it.

I drove past St. Joseph's Church and headed to Ivar's, one of his favorite restaurants. There were a lot of boats in the harbor. Gazing out at the water and munching on French fries, I noticed a homeless man digging through a trash bin. My reverie about the past gave way to concern about the problems of the present day. I gave the man some money and said, "Please go buy yourself some food."

He thanked me as he put the money in his pocket, then

continued looking through the trash. "The food in here is still good," he said.

I took it as a sign it was time to let go of the past for now and head home.

It had been a good day. I felt closer to my birth father after seeing where he had spent so many years of his life. By all accounts, they had been happy years. Visiting my mother's old school had been a bonus.

There were still so many questions to be answered. Did Tom know about me? Why hadn't Patsy and Tom married? Why hadn't my adoptive parents told me the truth?

But those questions would all have to wait for another day. I drove home with a light heart and a feeling of peace.

CHAPTER TWELVE

My journey to discover the truth about my birth had at times been exhausting and stressful, but it had also been joyful, as I discovered that my new family members were unusually kind people.

The first biological relative I "met" through the biotechnology site was my second cousin Mike. He spent many hours with me on the phone, not only patiently listening but eventually directing me to the Mahoney family. Not long after I met my father's birth family, Mike told me he would be traveling to Washington state on family business. I was excited to meet him and thank him in person for all he had done.

It was fitting that Mike's visit started off with a discussion about genealogy in my living room. He had been accompanied by his friend Dale, who had learned that he was a descendant of Daniel Boone, the famous American explorer and frontiersman. My daughter Leia volunteered that she had been told by one of her father's family members that she, too, was a descendant of Daniel Boone. I marveled at what a small world it really was and wondered if one day we might discover that Leia and Dale were actually related.

In the 1990s the house next door was a "party house,"

rented by college students who frequently invited local bands to play. One of the bands that played at the house a few times was Nirvana. I don't remember specifically hearing Kurt Cobain singing "Smells Like Teen Spirit" or any of their other hits, but when they signed a recording contract and became famous, it was the talk of the neighborhood. I enjoyed telling Mike the story because he was an avid Nirvana fan as well as a talented musician. He and Dale were eager to visit the house where Kurt Cobain and his bandmate Dave Grohl lived, which was just a few blocks away.

At a local waterfront restaurant, we bonded even more over dinner. Mike shared that his closest family members lived in southern California, and they weren't in touch much these days with their Mahoney relatives in Washington. In fact, my birth father Tom had been the conduit between the families, traveling back and forth with the latest news and, of course, an endless supply of photographs. He usually brought his harmonica and spent hours entertaining the children.

Hearing Mike speak so highly of Tom filled me with pride. Despite not having a family of his own, he was clearly a family man. I had yet to hear anyone say an unkind thing about him.

When Mike invited me to visit the family in southern California and said he'd love to reconnect with the northwestern Mahoneys, I realized that "the ripple effect" of DNA testing was once again taking place. Mike's search had led to me and vice versa, and our stories were prompting more family members to want to reconnect after decades of being out of touch.

Now I, like my father, had the chance to be a link between the families.

I told Mike about the get-together being planned by

Joe Mahoney's daughter Maria, the cousin I had originally thought might be my sister. (We were calling it the "Cousin Fest.") I was disappointed that he couldn't attend the event due to work obligations. When he invited me to San Diego to meet the "SoCal" side of the family, I eagerly agreed. A few months ago we were unknown to each other; now I considered us good friends. Even though my trip would probably not take place for many months, I was looking forward to it.

All my birth father's siblings had passed away, so I appreciated any information that his other relatives might be able to share with me. So far nearly everything I knew about his life had come from his nephews, Tim and Mike. I was looking forward to Maria's "Cousin Fest," which would be another opportunity to learn more about Tom.

My son Jesse was flying in from Colorado. "Another chance to feel our DNA humming!" he joked.

"You might be right about that," I said. I was glad my daughter Leia would be there, too.

Maria and her husband were hosting the get-together. They greeted us warmly when we arrived, and Maria introduced us to her sisters and several other cousins from the Mahoney family. They all remembered Tom and were eager to share stories with me.

"He was so intelligent. So knowledgeable about a lot of different things."

"I remember that he was always taking pictures. And he loved to play the harmonica."

"He was a big history buff."

Tom had been a veteran, and I was touched when Maria presented me with his military uniforms and the flag from his funeral.

Of course there were pictures. A number of them

showed Tom with different women, so he had obviously had relationships besides the one he had with my mother. It remained a mystery how long his relationship with Patsy had lasted. No one seemed to know. My uncle Sean had met him a couple of times and my half-brother Mark had said he thought it was very brief. Maria and my cousins had no idea. They just remembered how devoted he was to family.

For the first time I was able to see my father in a video. It had been taken at Maria's wedding, and at one point Tom was attempting to take a picture of the bride when one of his brothers got in the way. Tom pulled on his brother's sweater and everyone laughed. It was only a short clip, but I was glued to the screen, looking for signs of resemblance or mannerisms.

"Those two were always bickering or interrupting each other," one of the cousins said with a laugh.

All these insights into my father's life were priceless, but the gift I cherished most was the collection of stories that Tom had written himself. His love for storytelling and his ability to connect with children were both put to good use when he volunteered at the local school and shared those stories.

"What Tom Learned in Life" was one of them.

"First, early in life we have to learn to get along with one another regardless of where we come from. Having an open mind, we can communicate and learn from one another's experiences. Respect each other and don't dwell on each other's shortcomings. We should all try to help one another when we can and share our experiences in life.

"Sometimes I learned these things the hard way. By being tolerant, fair and honest in our dealings with

others, we can become leaders and train others to get along well in this world.

"When we gather all these lessons and abide by them, we can all live together in a happier world."

Maria gave me a picture of Tom in a classroom full of children. I can only imagine how popular he must have been with them and could easily picture him pulling his harmonica out of his pocket between stories. I was pleased that "What Tom Learned in Life" reflected my own personal values.

"Oh, I can't wait to read the rest of his stories," I said. "To be able to read his own words is such a gift. Thank you."

The stories of my father transitioned into stories of my grandfather, Neil Mahoney.

I listened, fascinated, as my cousins told a tale of mobsters, a man on the run, and an appeal to one of the most famous politicians in the country.

CHAPTER THIRTEEN

In the 1940s, Neil Mahoney was a successful attorney practicing in Buffalo, New York. At that time organized crime families and mobsters controlled much of New York.

According to family lore and seemingly backed up by a letter from 1944 that had been preserved for nearly eighty years, Neil Mahoney was pressured to defend a potential client with ties to organized crime. He refused, quickly reaching the conclusion that if he remained in New York, his own life and that of his family would be in danger.

So he headed for Seattle.

On the other side of the country, Neil thought they would be safe and he would be able to resume his law practice. Unfortunately, that was not the case. Promising job offers were mysteriously withdrawn—if it even came to the point of an offer.

Frustrated, Neil wrote a lengthy missive to Thomas Dewey. I was given a copy of his letter.

September 30, 1944

Hon. Thomas E. Dewey,
  The Capitol,
  Albany, N.Y.

Dear Sir:

In the first instance it may seem presumptuous to address a communication of this kind to you, one of exalted position in this fair land of ours, especially in the midst of the Presidential campaign but after sober reflection on the facts as hereinafter set forth, probably not.

The inspiration to do so comes from some of your speeches heard over the radio on your late tour of the west coast in which you stated that it had been a pleasure to meet all types of the American people and to discuss their problems with them.

It has become increasingly evident that among a vast number of citizens of all ranks in life the name and personality of Thomas E. Dewey has become an outstanding symbol of sincerity, integrity and force in public life for the good of the nation and its people individually and collectively.

As one of this great number the writer has discussed a great many times your work as prosecutor and executive and has repeatedly emphasized the huge benefits derived by the people of this country as the result of your fine job in putting an end to the conspiracies and rackets in New York, by means of which the God given rights of a great many people to live without malicious hindrance, annoyances and even injuries to person and property, had been trampled upon for a long time.

Accent has been placed in most of your recent addresses on the matter of jobs, especially for returning service men and your expressed purpose and intention to see that every man who is fit, able and willing to work is provided with a job by means of which he may earn a living and support himself and his family if he has one. This is usually applied to the period after the war. This problem now and has been for a long time how to get men for the jobs, or at least it is supposed to be.

But, strange as it may seem, the problem of your correspondent has been for almost three years, lack of a job, lack of an income for himself and family including seven children, five of whom have been dependent for most that period, tho at all time in good health, possessed of ability and energy and ready and eager to work.

There must be and is a reason. The facts which make the case are as follows: The writer is a member of your own profession, a lawyer. Starting at scratch after admission to the New York Bar about thirty years ago, overcoming many obstacles and difficulties, a successful practice in Buffalo was attained the hard way and continued for many years: also a high standing at the bar.

About eight years ago thru a new corporation client and in the roll *[sic]* of one of its representatives tho not an official, a "character" from afar was injected into the picture and very shortly assumed the role of practices and representing a philosophy of life, business and modus operandi utterly foreign to my practice. The choice was presented in effect, either take it and like it if you want to survive or its *[sic]* your finish. I did neither but gave them a fight and good one. These developments ran along between 1936 and 1938.

I stopped reading at this point to consider his words: *either take it and like it if you want to survive or it's your finish. I did neither but gave them a fight and a good one.*

There were several paragraphs detailing lawsuits, "veiled threats," "mysterious obstacles," and the sudden loss of clients. Neil closed his practice and applied for numerous jobs on the East Coast, to no avail. One job in Albany was offered and subsequently withdrawn with the cryptic comment, "Nothing doing." Neil continued his litany about how the Mahoneys were suffering financially.

For more than three years it was necessary to live for the most part on accumulated assets and to incur debt to carry on. Bitter suffering and distress was caused to my family and finally in the summer of 1943 our home was lost and we were compelled to vacate it.

Coming to Seattle at a time when the law business was going strong and lawyers to handle the work scarce I obtained a place with a reputable firm at a moderate salary with a nondetermined tenure but a fair possibility of becoming permanent. A large furnished house was leased for a year and something in the way of home life was resumed after shifting around for three months. It was also possible to resume schooling for four of the children and something in the way of normal life was restored.

After a few months an application for admission to the Washington State Bar on motion was filed and after detailed investigation and oral questioning before the Board of Governors it was approved and I was sworn in in July. Tho limited for the most part while not admitted to briefing the work done was commended by the firm as good and in at least one important federal tax case decided in favor of the office client the court in its opinion stated that the briefs submitted had been very able. But with the suggestion that I might do better elsewhere came separation from the payroll two months ago and tho on good authority there still exists a demand for good legal assistants here there has been nothing doing in the way of a job except in one instance where a job was promised and shortly afterward withdrawn.

Now, the facts as you can readily see all add up. While up to date no evidence had been made available to support a cause of action in court (and as usual in circumstances of this kind people "know nothing about it, etc. etc.") there has existed for a long time a determined and widespread purpose on the part of at least two or more persons to prevent a man from getting a job and to get him out of it if he gets one. This of course under the law constitutes a conspiracy and its very essence is malicious, damage necessarily following. The financial loss has been large but by far the most dastardly effects of it have been blighted lives of growing children, interruptions in education, a broken home and destruction of peace of mind over a long period.

The question which is up for determination at this time is whether this vicious conspiracy is to be permitted to continue with its dastardly effects and whether my newly established home far away in the northwest is also to be broken up and my family scattered for the want of a place to live and the means to maintain life.

The facts are submitted to you as the man who has fought and conquered the most vicious conspiracies and rackets in America and as one who has stated publicly within the month that is your purpose and intention to see that every man fit and able to and willing to work has a job. I am in good health, active and alert in mind and body and like hard work and lots of it especially that of my profession and yet have been idle for long periods during the past three years with more work to be done than ever before in history.

If the Gestapo methods of Hitler Germany are to prevail in

America where is our freedom and what are we fighting for? Two of my nephews are in the army in France, one already wounded in action, one is with the Marines in the South Pacific and I have one son in Preflight training with the army air force in California. This constitutes 100% of those of my immediate family of military age and physically fit. Are their efforts and sacrifices for freedom to be in vain?

Here I rest my case.

Respectfully yours,

(Signed by Neil Mahoney)

*****

Mr. Dewey, who would go on to become governor of New York and run against Harry S. Truman for the office of president, never replied to my grandfather's letter. Neil Mahoney secured a few legal jobs but never was able to establish the kind of successful practice he had in Buffalo. He eventually retired in Seattle.

Had my grandfather not been a man of integrity, had he taken on the troublesome case in question and remained in New York, his son Tom and Patsy—my birth parents—never would have met. The power of one decision to affect the future of so many descendants was truly mind-boggling. By the grace of God, my parents had crossed paths in Seattle and created me.

One more interesting tidbit was shared with me about Neil's wife, my grandmother. Her father had been a New York Assemblyman, and in 1927 he was one of the first people to cross the famous Peace Bridge between Canada and the United States (linking Ontario and New York).

I felt a sense of pride when I learned about the

Mahoney family history. It was just beginning to sink in that it was my history, too.

The time went by far too fast. There were other home videos with Tom, and Maria assured me we would watch them together in the future. After a wonderful meal, Maria and the others presented me with flowers and a wall hanging with the inscription:

Family

means you are part

of something beautiful

and you will be loved unconditionally

no matter what

My children and I departed with the feeling that once again, we had been treated with incredible kindness.

I stayed up late, reading my birth father's stories, told in his own words.

CHAPTER FOURTEEN

Tom wrote the way he apparently told stories—in a meandering fashion, determined to include even the smallest detail. I was becoming more convinced he was in many ways the polar opposite of my birth mother, Patsy. There were no priests or nuns keeping an eye on him or measuring his IQ when he was a child. Even then, he was a free spirit.

"Being one of eight children, I got tired of seeing everything in the back yard. So, when I was four years old, I decided to go out and explore the world. I went out through the gate and headed down to the corner, passing a vacant lot next to our house. When I got to the corner, I crossed the street and headed west.

"It was getting to be a really hot afternoon and I noticed along the curb that the patches of tar were starting to bubble from the heat. I grabbed a popsicle stick and started digging into the soft tar. When I got a clump of tar, I would pull it off the stick and mold it like clay. I was two miles away from home but didn't really think I was lost. I was having fun with what I was doing. I made three or four of the tar balls and wanted to take them home to use them for xylophone sticks. I was

sweating and had black tar all over my face, shirt, and hands.

"Finally, I decided that I had enough of that. I went a little farther to see what else I could find, then realized I was a long way from home. After being gone for about two hours, my parents sent people out to search for me. I heard a car pull up and the driver said, 'Do you live on 55 Winston Road? Your parents are worried sick about you.' The man took me home and my mother took me in and scolded the heck out of me. 'Just look at you with your dirty hands and shirt. Where were you?' I said, 'I was down the street digging in tar.' My mother replied, 'Well, I don't know how I'm going to get that tar out of your shirt!'"

It was a simple story, but one nearly every little kid could relate to. Who didn't try to make a break for it when they were about three or four years old? He gave older children a glimpse into the past with another tale, entitled "Troubles I Got into at School."

"In the early days of high school, many of us rode our bicycles to school and parked them underneath the football stands. There was one student who brought carrier pigeons in a box on his bike. These pigeons had little metal canisters attached to their legs where you could put little messages in. He would release the pigeons and they would circle up and head back to his home roost in his attic. During World War 1 the Army Signal Corps used homing pigeons to send messages back to headquarters. A battalion was lost in the Argon and if it wasn't for the homing pigeons carrying a vital message, they never would have been able to rescue them. Three of us were late to class that day and were

sent down to the assistant principal's office, where we got a strict lecture on being punctual.

"One day a couple of us decided that we didn't want to go to school, so we took a streetcar downtown where we would go to the back of a movie theater. We climbed the exit stairs to the upper level balcony and waited for somebody to come out of the exit so that we could go in. That particular day, the truant officer was just inside the door and caught us. We were suspended for three days and our parents had to report to the school. Fortunately, I got off easy because I had just completed a model airplane which the truant officer admired. He said, 'Just keep working on projects like that and stay out of trouble.'

"Did you young students ever get into trouble? If you did, I'd like to hear about it and the punishment that you received. Always think twice and ask yourself, Is it worth it? Once you learn right from wrong and the consequences you might receive, you will always do right."

He always signed his writings, "Your Pal, Tom."

He wrote about family vacations spent in their summer cabin in Honey Harbor, near Toronto, Canada. He painted a picture of lazy days spent fishing for black bass and perch, surrounded by snapping turtles and bullfrogs. He captured images of bonfires and roasting hot dogs and marshmallows. Picking blueberries and feasting on blueberry pie with a scoop of ice cream on top. Swimming and exploring the Canadian woods.

Even as a child he must have been a history buff because he wrote about visiting Fort Saint Marie in Ontario on the way to the family cabin. The French

Jesuit settlement was established in 1649 and subsequent conflicts involving missionary activity, the spread of infectious diseases, and rivalry between Indian nations eventually led to the killing of eight Jesuit missionaries. These trips must have helped him cultivate his curious nature.

I could only imagine how he might have held the attention of elementary school students when he shared his detailed story of the one-room schoolhouse near Honey Harbor, which was only accessible by boat. The students were half French and half Indian, and they adored their dedicated teacher, George, who walked over rocks in the water to get to school every morning and fire up the two potbellied stoves before launching into the day's lessons (conducted in French).

In another story he recalled how he returned—*"Years later I ran 250 miles away up into Canada to a place called Honey Harbor"*—and met up with an old friend from his youth, who had retired in the area. They spent two glorious days traveling the waterways as Tom learned how to navigate and read channel markers. What had he been "running away" from? I wondered. He was indeed another Jack Kerouac, as his nephew Tim had proclaimed.

Through yet another story I learned that at the end of 1944, he had attended aerial gunning school at Tyndall Field in northwest Florida. He recounted being in the back turret during a training mission, fifty miles off the Gulf Coast, where he witnessed another plane's engine catch fire. The crew was ordered to bail out over water, but the young pilot decided to try to save the plane. He crashed upon landing and died.

When "VE Day" was declared in 1945, signaling the end of the war, Tom hitchhiked back to Seattle. As he recounted his adventures, I felt as if I were right there with him, taking rides from trucks full of soldiers before hooking up with some fellows headed to California to pick up a wanted felon, enjoying a complimentary whiskey and ginger ale offered by a young woman by the side of a road in eastern Oregon, touring Navy ships docked in Portland and conversing with pilots who had flown missions in the Pacific and over Japan, and finally, taking a train to rejoin his family in Seattle.

One story that made me feel close to Tom took place a decade before my birth. He purchased one of the only two Monarch motorbikes available in Seattle in preparation for a trip down the Oregon coast. Near Raymond, Washington, he encountered a huge forest fire, and he immediately offered his services as a volunteer firefighter.

"Some of those trees that were burning were cedar trees, eight to ten feet in diameter. My job was to take water to the radiator of a Caterpillar that was being used to build a perimeter road around the fire. After the fire was put out, I headed south, across the Columbia River, and on to Tillamook, Oregon."

He took on various odd jobs during his six weeks on the road—picking pears and tomatoes, working cold storage, and whatever else paid a few bucks. I could envision him among the Sea Lion Caves near Depoe Bay, the farmlands in the Sacramento Valley, and driving his motorbike through the Siskiyou Mountains.

His rambling trek to California and back had special significance since I had made that trip myself so many times, especially during my childhood. My adoptive father Wayne was in the military and his assignments rotated between bases in Washington state and California. I had also spent time near Raymond, Washington, and, like Tom, had toured the famous cheese and ice cream factory in Tillamook, Oregon.

I didn't read all my birth father's stories that evening, but I read enough of them to understand that he had an independent, adventurous spirit and loved people.

I was thankful he had passed those qualities on to me through his DNA. My own DNA was "humming" as I fell asleep.

CHAPTER FIFTEEN

The months were flying by and it seemed as if I was receiving new information about my birth parents and my newly discovered biological relatives on a near-daily basis. At the same time, I was constantly revisiting my past in my head. Trying to reframe nearly sixty years of my life was emotionally exhausting. I was obsessed, and the obsession was wreaking havoc with my sleep patterns as well as my overall health. I had always been a perfectionist, but I had begun making mistakes at work.

At the end of 2018, I made the difficult decision to resign from my government job and work part time. I realized after speaking with a counselor that I was suffering from the effects of trauma. There are many different types of trauma, and for me, learning that my parents were not my biological parents had been traumatizing. In addition, I was still grieving the death of my father Wayne, whom I loved dearly.

Working part time allowed me to catch my breath and try to restore some balance in my life. I also needed to reexamine my health in light of what I had learned about my birth family's medical history, which was much different from that of my adoptive family.

For much of my life, my weight had been an issue.

My adoptive mother Bernadette was a petite woman who couldn't seem to hide her dismay that I had a larger frame. At age sixteen she gave me a hope chest with her size three wedding dress inside.

"I want you to be married in this dress," she said, despite the fact that I was already too big to fit into it.

I was put on strict diets as a teenager and dropped several dress sizes, which pleased my parents—especially my mother. However, I soon found myself unable to finish playing a game of tennis or participate in any other sport I had previously enjoyed. When I needed to have my tonsils removed, the doctor informed my mother that I was so severely malnourished that he was afraid that I might not wake up if they gave me general anesthesia. Instead, they had to remove my tonsils under local anesthesia.

I didn't start feeling healthy until my late teens, when I married, moved out, and gained control of my own body again. I didn't worry too much about gaining weight back because the older women in my parents' families all seemed very healthy in spite of their extra pounds. When I discovered I was adopted, however, I had to take a fresh look at how my true genetics might affect my health in the future.

My birth mother had been obese when she died in her late fifties. She had a specific condition that had developed in adulthood and contributed to her death. Learning about this was a wake-up call for me. I did not want to develop the same condition and die early.

I decided to lose weight—this time not to please someone else but to honor myself and my body. I embarked on an exercise and weight-loss program, something I would not have been able to do had I kept working full time.

I also began writing a book about my adoption story. Between working on my book, devoting time to improving my health, continuing to connect with relatives, trying to process my past, and working part time, I was still very busy, but I was slowly gaining control of the situation and setting goals rather than simply reacting. I began to feel more grounded.

There were still difficult times, though, especially as I tried to process my past. Memories would spring to mind even when I was trying not to think about them.

"You never want to have just one child," my father said sarcastically to my mother one day when my brother and I were fighting. "You always want to have at least two children." Was there a meaning behind those words? I wondered. Did he only want one child and perhaps my mother insisted on adopting a second one? Was his sarcastic tone because he was repeating something she had said?

"Bernadette, we should have stuck to raising dogs. It was easier." Again, I wondered if he had really wanted me.

"Blood is thicker than water." This was said more than once in my house. Why would someone who adopted a child say such a thing?

I recalled times when I would lay my head against my mother's shoulder as we sat on the sofa. "Don't lean on me," she would say, pushing me away. I didn't understand why a mother would do that. Did she ever feel a connection to me?

My relationship with my parents had always seemed different from those of my friends in our close-knit neighborhood. I had always shrugged it off, putting it down to the four very different personalities in my household. Now I was putting every memory under a microscope. How much of how I was raised might be attributed to the fact that I was adopted and how much might have been due to questionable parenting skills?

It was frustrating to know I would never have answers to these questions.

CHAPTER SIXTEEN

As a child, I was taught the importance of knowing and respecting my family history. The woman I grew up believing was my paternal grandmother came from a family that kept volumes of history about themselves—chronicles that predated the Civil War. They regularly produced a family newsletter, and for nearly seventy years they had held festive annual family reunions, usually near the Wallowa Lake area of eastern Oregon. Many of the men wore cowboy hats, some of the women sold family cookbooks, and without fail there was an auction of a mincemeat pie.

My adoptive father Wayne told me his mother Norma's family arrived in eastern Oregon from New Mexico via wagon train. The three brothers who would become the family patriarchs settled in a small town called Troy, and one of them fathered my grandmother Norma. As soon as she finished the eighth grade, Norma became a schoolteacher.

Norma would eventually marry a young man named Lute. Lute's father, Michael, had only been thirteen years old when he snuck aboard a boat that was departing Germany for the United States. He made his way out west, where he homesteaded farms in Oregon. With the help of his sons, he'd fix one place up, sell it, and go on to the next one.

Michael's son Lute was a farmer living in Elgin, Oregon, when he married Norma. They had several children, including my father, Wayne.

This was the foundation upon which my identity had been built. I was part of a large clan who knew exactly who they were and where they had come from. And they took great pride in that knowledge.

Once I married and had children of my own, attending the family reunions became more difficult. Nonetheless, my children were raised to respect their family history, just as I was. My son Jesse was fascinated by the story of his great-great-grandfather Michael, who had come to America as a stowaway. Jesse proudly wrote a school paper about his brave and courageous ancestor.

The last family reunion I attended took place about four years before I discovered I had been adopted. At that time in my life, I was experiencing a feeling I could only describe as "unsettled."

"You have some blind spots," a friend told me at the time. She often used the term "blind spots" when I would tell her about odd things that didn't make sense. "You have things in your life that don't add up. Something is missing, but you don't know what it is."

I didn't know what to say to her. I could not explain my unease.

I attended the family reunion in the remote, tiny town of Troy, Oregon, with my Aunt Diana, who had entered our family as a foster child. Her daughter Julie had come along for the reunion, too. As the car bounced around on the rugged dirt road that seemed to go forever, I thought about my grandmother Norma and what her life might have been like as the "schoolteacher of record" for the

Lost Prairie School in Flora, Oregon—now a ghost town somewhere on a nearby butte.

We came to a sign hammered into a tree that pointed to "Troy" in one direction and "Promise" in another. At one point we sat in the car and waited patiently as a herd of elk slowly made its way across the dirt road.

Upon our arrival, I was given a nametag that traced my lineage: BEN – NORMA – WAYNE. My aunt's nametag said: BEN – NORMA – DIANA. Our nametags proclaimed our connection to the family.

Everyone I met was very pleasant and seemed eager to talk about my grandmother, Norma. I could see a strong family resemblance among many of my relatives, but I didn't see anyone who looked like me.

Even so, the question of adoption never entered my mind. There was always the chance my feeling of not belonging was simply due to the lack of close contact with most of the relatives in adulthood.

If I had been raised in a family that was not so steeped in their heritage, one that did not place such emphasis on a shared history and family lore, perhaps finding out I was adopted might have been less of a shock. Perhaps if I hadn't been raised in a family where honesty was a core value—ranking right up there with hard work—I might not have felt the confusion and, yes, even anger that I found myself battling once I learned I was not "blood."

"In all things the truth is always the best policy," my mother Bernadette used to say. My father echoed these sentiments throughout my childhood.

Yet they had not only withheld the truth from me, they had vigorously encouraged me to believe a lie.

And my relatives—who were and still are very nice people—had gone along with it. At least until it came to creating a family tree.

After I discovered I was adopted, one of my cousins confided that after the reunion in Troy, I had been the subject of a heated discussion. There was a dispute about whether or not to include me on the family tree. Some wanted to include my name but add "adopted" (even though I didn't know I was adopted at the time). Others wanted to include my name like they did with Aunt Diana. It was finally decided to leave the space under my father Wayne's name... blank.

Blank. Just like on my birth certificate.

When I heard this, I was shocked. I was happy I didn't know about the family tree until after I had met and been embraced by my birth family. By that time, I had experienced the "humming of my DNA" and felt the joy of being accepted for exactly who I was.

"You're so much like Uncle Sean that I can't believe it," my son Jesse told me. While my adoptive parents were always telling me to "settle down now" and not get too excited or too loud, my birth family seemed not to notice when I laughed too much or seemed too enthusiastic. No one told Uncle Sean to settle down.

Processing my feelings toward my adoptive family was going to take some time. From outward appearances, nothing much had changed. My cousins were still my cousins and excluding the matter of the family tree, no one treated me any differently once the lie was exposed. The struggle was not outward but inward, and it required all the forgiveness and grace I could muster.

CHAPTER SEVENTEEN

My mother Bernadette was a front-row parishioner in the Catholic Church. The word that always springs to mind when I'm asked to describe her is "staunch."

She came by her devotion to duty and the Catholic Church honestly. Her mother, my grandmother Peggy, was also active in the church. She had statues of saints placed throughout the house, and she spent a lot of time lighting candles and praying to those saints. I remember how she would arise very early in the morning and make breakfast for her husband, whom she called "Daddy." Then she would sit at the kitchen table and watch the many birds that flocked to the back yard to fill up on birdseed. When I visited, she would let me have a small amount of coffee and watch the birds with her. The rest of Peggy's day was spent making sure her house was immaculate and the yard was well manicured. Appearances were very important.

My mother married my father Wayne while he was serving in the military. He was a veteran of the Korean and Vietnam wars. I have memories of living in both Washington state and California, depending on his stateside assignments.

My father was not raised in the Catholic Church;

rather, he grew up with his mother Norma's faith, a belief in the concept of universal salvation. Norma was an educated woman who learned both Greek and Hebrew and helped translate scripture for Concordant Publishing, which was dedicated to providing accurate translation of the original scriptures. She did this in addition to teaching school in rural eastern Oregon.

My father converted to Catholicism when he married my mother, but he did not completely disavow what his mother Norma had taught him. I loved the times my father and I were able to discuss religion, usually when my mother was away. The main doctrine of universal salvation—that instead of eternal damnation and suffering, all spirits will eventually be able to live in harmony with the creator—was appealing to me, but I didn't dare express an opinion or a preference. Perhaps that was because I was desperate to be loved and was somewhat of a "people pleaser." As I entered adulthood, both Catholicism and the idea of universal salvation influenced the development of my own spiritual beliefs.

My parents were well respected in our middle-class community. After he retired from the military, my father worked as a welder and boilermaker. Both my parents were active in the Lions Club and my mother volunteered with the Catholic Church. Most of their leisure time was spent with their friends, playing cards, going out to dinner, bowling, and boating.

I have fond memories of my great-grandfather Sam, who had a strawberry farm. He had an enormous mustache and used to tickle my neck with it until I squealed. My grandfather Frank was a great jokester. These relatives treated me as if I were an important part of the family, never letting on that they were not biologically related to me at all. At the same time, I noticed early in life that I was very different from my cousins, who seemed born to ride horses and embrace outdoor activities with ease. My physiology lent itself to getting thrown off a horse, not riding one.

A favorite relative of mine was my mother's brother, who lived in California. It was his children who sent the letter informing me I was adopted. I had always loved spending time with my uncle and his family, listening to his entertaining stories. Knowing that during all those visits, my uncle and his family had known the secret of my birth was another factor I would need time to process.

My relationship with my mother was never close, but not so abnormal as to cause me to question my parentage. I was envious of some of the girls in our close-knit neighborhood who seemed to have better relationships with their moms. No one had a perfect life, though, and it was sharing our experiences and helping each other get through rough times that bonded our little circle together so tightly. With an emotionally unavailable mother and a father I couldn't always count on, the families in my neighborhood were like wagons of compassion that surrounded me protectively.

Even though my mother Bernadette had been raised in a house that was perpetually spotless, she had a weakness that she shared with my father. They were both "pack rats." (Nowadays they would probably be called "hoarders.") I spent a great deal of time, especially during my teenage years, cleaning up the clutter and trying to make our house presentable to visitors. Nearly all the household chores fell on my shoulders, and many times a friend would have to pitch in and help me get things done so I could join in on activities with the group. When I wanted to join the drill team, a neighbor mom persuaded my parents to allow it on the condition that she would transport me to practice and events along with her own daughter.

I was "the good child" who rarely got into trouble, brought home mostly As on my report card, and followed my mother's strict rules. Sometimes I felt as if my role in the family was to be the person pounding the sign in the front yard that said, "Everything is okay here."

I wanted to go to college, but that was not an option. "We are working-class people," my father said. He had struggled in school and perhaps because of his own difficulties, he didn't see the value of higher education. My mother was adamant that I needed to follow in her footsteps: get married, stay home, and take care of the family. Years later, when I self-financed my own education, attending classes while working thirty hours a week, they were still unsupportive. They just had a different mentality when it came to people's—especially women's—roles in life.

What bothered me more than the lack of enthusiasm surrounding my own college graduation was the lukewarm response my son received when he earned his master's degree in geophysics engineering. After the truth about my adoption came out, Jesse shared his own memory. "He just didn't seem proud of me like a man should be proud of his grandson." I hurt for my son when I heard that.

I didn't realize until my mother passed away that she had been the real backbone of the family, in spite of her obvious battle with depression. When she wasn't busy doing something productive for the church, she spent a lot of time on the couch, watching TV. Maybe it took a lot of energy to keep so many secrets.

Why had my parents adopted me? Had adopting me really brought my stern mother any happiness or had she just been fulfilling a "duty" to the church? Which memories would it benefit me to analyze and which ones could I simply "let go"? In early 2019 many questions along these lines filled my head, day and night, as I tried to create a new, healthier life for myself, both physically and emotionally.

It would take time to gain some closure, I realized. The foundation of my existence had been ripped out of the ground and needed to be replaced with a new, stronger one.

CHAPTER EIGHTEEN

Easter was approaching, so I sent cards to some of my new relatives—the ones that I had the most contact with. They had been good about keeping in touch, mailing and texting me photos of my birth parents. I was thankful family members on both my mother's and father's sides had accumulated so many pictures and writings that they were willing to share with me.

One new cousin, Jim, even invited me to his home to watch some home movies he had that Tom had been in. Even brief glimpses of my father in action meant a lot to me. I was also touched when Jim presented me with one of Tom's harmonicas. I had seen several photos of Tom with his harmonica, my favorite being the one with a little boy sitting on the sofa next to him. I wondered what tune he had been playing to entertain him.

I was grateful for many other documents that came my way. My cousin Desmond in California sent me a 1926 calendar from the "Marguerite Confectionary" in Vancouver, British Columbia—the candy store owned by my birth mother Patsy's grandfather. He also sent me baptism records and a family tree.

"Found a few more pics of Mahoney family that Tom had sent us over the years. Thought some would be good for your family album. Lots of airplanes! Quite a character. Always in a good mood."

These photos came from Kit, the widowed mother of my newfound second cousin, Mike. Kit had been adopted and it was Mike's search for her relatives that enabled us to connect through the biotechnology website.

Kit's late husband, Dave, was my father Tom's nephew. Dave had credited Tom for encouraging him to become a pilot. When Dave was a baby, Tom bought the toy airplanes that hung over his crib and later worked on model planes with him.

On a visit to the San Juan Islands with a friend, I was able to meet Kit and her daughter. Despite the fact that her son was trying to locate blood relatives, Kit herself had no interest in finding her birth parents. She had discovered she was adopted at age twenty-one when she applied for a marriage license and was told she needed her birth certificate. The discovery was a surprise, but Kit decided to take a different path forward than I did.

"I could not have had a better childhood," she said. "I don't have any desire to find any answers and I don't have anything to resolve." It was hard for me to understand how she could learn she was adopted and then just go on with her life.

She asked me an interesting question. Was I just looking for information about my birth family or did I need a connection?

The truth was, I probably needed both. But there was another factor at play. I had been raised in a family that emphasized—more than most families—the importance of knowing about one's ancestry. It was so much a part of my psychological makeup that I couldn't fathom *not* trying to find out about my roots.

I was gratified when Kit told me I had Tom's nose and eyes and touched when she said she thought he would be proud of me.

My friend and I enjoyed exploring the island. At sunset we found ourselves near a lighthouse that was bathed in beautiful, waning rays of light. Once again, I felt a connection to God, who kept reminding me of His presence on my journey.

My conversation with Kit elicited a memory from my childhood. We were living in California at the time. My brother and I were sitting in the back seat of a car being driven by my father, and my father's friend Bob was sitting in the front passenger seat.

"Say, kids, I have a question for you." My father turned his head slightly to the right and raised his voice a bit. "Bob here has a son who was adopted when he was a baby. They told him he was adopted when he old enough to understand. What do you think about that? If you were adopted, would you rather know you were adopted or not know?"

My brother said he'd rather not know. I said I would rather know, which prompted my brother to try to convince me why it would be better not to know. I don't recall his reasoning, but eventually I agreed with him.

It never occurred to either one of us to wonder why our father would ask us such a question. In hindsight it seems likely that he had discussed the issue with his friend Bob and Bob had urged him to tell us the truth.

A study was published that indicated about two-thirds of teenaged adoptees want to meet their birth parents, and nearly three-quarters want to know why they were given up for adoption.

I was very well aware that despite the crushing discovery that my birth parents were dead, my journey to find them had brought more joy than pain into my life. Not every reunion story has a happy ending. And many adoptees never learn "why" they were given to strangers to raise.

There is no one right answer to the question of whether it benefits an adoptee to find their biological parents. In the U.S. alone, there are about five million different answers to that question, because that's how many adopted children there are in this country.

For me the answer to the question was an unequivocal "yes." Finding my biological family had been a tremendous benefit to my life in ways I was just beginning to really understand.

CHAPTER NINETEEN

It had been a year since I discovered I was adopted. My daughter Leia and I took a road trip to a seaside town on the Olympic Peninsula to commemorate the occasion, enjoying dinner on the deck of a popular seafood restaurant as the sun shone brightly. We talked about how our lives had changed during the past year and how the discovery of a whole new family had impacted us emotionally.

As we waited for our meals to arrive, I texted my cousin Kevin, whose letter had started me on my journey on this day in 2018. *"What an amazing and enlightening year it has been,"* he responded. Earlier he had been intrigued by what I had written about the humming of our cells. *"I have a strong sense of this at times and have been thinking about this phenomenon lately."* Another "ripple effect"—I was prompting my adoptive relatives to consider an aspect of family that had never occurred to them.

Leia and I talked about the upcoming family gathering of my birth mother Patsy's relatives. This time there would be many more Eberhardts in attendance, and it would be held at my uncle Rick's lakeside home. My son Jesse was planning to fly in from Colorado.

A few days before the event, an odd and rather spooky incident occurred. I glanced in the bathroom mirror, my head slightly turned, and I caught a glimpse of my profile. Only it wasn't my profile—it was my birth father's. I shifted my gaze and saw my birth mother's forehead and hair. What was happening? Was I crazy or was I manifesting my subconscious struggle with figuring out my true identity? I closed my eyes for a moment and when I opened them, I saw myself again. The next time this happened, I concluded that my psyche was integrating the multiple images of my parents that I had pored over so carefully these past few months.

My cousin Kim, who had hosted the first Eberhardt soiree, suggested what I could bring to Rick's party and how to dress. When I told her how I felt the "humming in my cells" at the previous event and wondered if I would feel it again, she laughed and said, "You're not going to feel a hum because it's going to be a nuclear explosion." I hoped she was right, but I wanted to stay objective.

My adoptive mother Bernadette had always been adamant about the importance of punctuality, and tardiness on anyone's part could possibly ruin not only the enjoyment of an event but the entire day. So when Jesse, Leia, and I encountered high volumes of traffic on the freeway, my body automatically began to tense up. It looked like we were going to be late. I hoped this didn't mean we would leave a negative first impression.

"Relax, Mom," Jesse said. "Most people don't expect anyone to arrive right on time."

We found the house easily and were greeted warmly by Uncle Rick and his wife. It was warm enough to sit outdoors on the deck, but I was also thankful it was too cool for swimming. I wouldn't have to change into my bathing suit. There were at least a dozen children playing near the water or taking turns jumping on the large trampoline. A badminton game was in progress, and anyone who was interested could be treated to a boat ride on the lake. Jesse and Leia divided their time between listening to the family stories and participating in the younger folks' activities.

Rick entertained us with reminiscences about his travels to Europe on behalf of the large department store he owned in the 1970s. It was interesting to reframe my memories and consider that my enthusiasm for the popular "No Star Jeans" (a marketing counter to "Star Jeans") might have followed Rick's trip abroad to discover new trends. He also shared an adventure he and his wife Sue had on a trip to Tahiti during a snorkeling excursion. Their local guide dove into the water for a few moments and when he returned, he encouraged them to leave the small boat and take a look at the sharks in the water. Each wearing only a mask and snorkel, Rick and Sue dutifully complied but were terrified when they quickly realized their guide had "chummed" the water— which meant that an increasing number of hungry sharks were feeding on the chum beneath their boat. Their only protection was the rope they were holding onto. They scrambled back to safety in record time.

Uncle Sean began singing a song with "Chum, chum, chum, chum" as its main chorus. Everyone was laughing and the atmosphere was congenial and relaxed. Sean had brought "princess crowns" for the little girls, which he ceremoniously placed on their heads. There were crowns left over and I was honored when Sue placed one of them on my head. A picture was taken of me being "crowned" into the family.

The icing on the cake was when I met people who told me I looked like my birth mother Patsy.

It was a tradition for Lee Eberhardt to give a blessing at family gatherings:

Thank you, dear Lord

For all Thy many bountiful gifts.

Thank you first of all and most of all, for sending Jesus Christ to earth,

as our Savior and Way-shower.

For this is the finest gift

That could come to man

Throughout all time.

The son of God and the Brother of Man.

Thank you, dear Lord,

for all Thy many bountiful gifts.

Following this blessing, the poem written by my grandmother Mary ("A Mother's Reflection") was read. Then my cousin Kim shared a few family stories. The children paid close attention when she held up Mary's cookie jar and recounted its history.

The meal included a pasta dish made from one of Mary's original recipes, a favorite she made for family gatherings. It was delicious, and the recipe was shared with everyone.

After dinner I made my way down to the fire pit so I could watch the sun set. There was a magnificent weeping willow tree at the water's edge, some thirty to forty feet tall. When I met my half-brother and half-sister, they shared a lovely poem written by our birth mother, Patsy. It was about a weeping willow tree. I wondered if this was the tree that had inspired her poem.

"That weeping willow nearly died," my uncle Rick told me after I admired it. "We really loved that tree, so we all prayed for it and guess what? It came back to life."

A few family members gathered around the fire pit. At one point Sue, our hostess, asked me if the family who raised me had treated me well. I gave a neutral answer as I had no desire to dishonor Bernadette and Wayne, and I was still trying to work through my feelings. And it was true that I was grateful someone raised me when I was given up by Patsy.

It had been a perfect, warm summer day, but now a storm was headed our way. We could hear the rumble of thunder in the distance and the sky lit up seconds later. It was time to head indoors. I glanced toward the house and saw the silhouettes of people on the deck. A small group of my female cousins stood on the side porch.

"Hi, girly-girl cousins," I said as they surrounded me. It felt like a warm blanket on a cold night. My DNA was definitely humming.

As we headed home, I thought about a conversation I had with my uncle Rick earlier in the day.

"Do you know if my birth father Tom knew about me?" I asked.

"Yes, he did know about you," Rick replied. His knowledge came directly from his sister, my birth mother Patsy.

Another piece of the puzzle. My birth father had known of my existence but had obviously agreed to give me up for adoption. His relatives had painted a vivid picture of a man who was a dedicated wanderer but also a man who highly valued family and relationships. Yet as far as I knew, he had never tried to find his only biological child.

I tried not to let ruminations about the past overshadow the joy of the present day.

"Did you feel the humming today, Jesse?" I asked.

"Sure did, Mom," he said with a smile.

CHAPTER TWENTY

After a year of gathering facts about the circumstances surrounding my adoption, I had to face the brutal truth. Finding the answers to the "who" and the "how" of the matter was not going to provide me with the answers to the question: "Why?"

I could hazard a guess as to why my birth parents hadn't married. Their relationship was short-lived, and they were clearly very different people. I could imagine that compatibility would have been a major issue, even if they had been in love.

But why had my mother not kept me? Why hadn't I been given the life that my half-brother and half-sister enjoyed in California just a few short years later?

I would never be able to know exactly what was in Patsy's heart, but I could look at the circumstances around her pregnancy. She obviously did not see marriage to my father as an option. Legal abortion was not yet possible. In the late 1950s and early 1960s, adoption was socially acceptable; in fact, it was seen by society as a benevolent act to take in an unwanted child. Being an "unwed mother" would have been a heavy stigma. Possible pressure from the Catholic Church and her work on military installations might have factored into her decision, too.

"She loved you and it was so difficult to give you up," my uncle Sean told me. I learned that Patsy had met with Bernadette, who agreed to Patsy's request that I be named Patricia, after her. It was another way she showed her love.

It took time, but I felt I had received my answer to that particular "why?"

There were other "why's." Why had my adoptive parents adopted me? From all outward appearances they were "good" parents, but I grew up with the distinct impression that they did not really enjoy having children. Did Bernadette believe that it would be a "benevolent act" to adopt children?

And, of course, there was the "why" surrounding the secrecy.

During a springtime trip to visit my son in Colorado, we attended an exhibit at a local museum that featured Leonardo da Vinci's artistic contributions along with his many underappreciated inventions. I learned that he was born out of wedlock, so he was not permitted to use his father's name. (That's why he was called "Leonardo of Vinci," Vinci being the town where he lived.) This treatment of children born to unmarried mothers hadn't completely changed by the time I was conceived nearly five hundred years later. In thinking about my adoptive parents, I tried to consider that maybe the "why" was because they didn't want me to feel devalued in a society that still had traces of these beliefs.

For at least the past thirty years, every reputable authority on the subject has agreed that a child who is adopted should be told the truth at the appropriate time (which can vary). Not telling a child is widely viewed as setting them up to feel betrayed and lied to, to feel shame about their birth, and to cause serious problems in the relationship going forward. Children have a right to know who they are and to search for their birth parents if they choose to. And as a practical matter, with the advent of DNA testing and changing state laws regarding birth certificates, it's simply not possible to erase all evidence of a child's true parentage.

In the 1960s, however, the thinking was the opposite. Most children were never told they were adopted (unless it was obvious due to ethnicity), so I could understand to some extent why Bernadette and Wayne did not tell me I was adopted when I was young. But to keep the truth from me for five decades? I wasn't sure I could ever understand the "why" of that decision. If they had told me once I reached adulthood, we would have had a chance to talk about it and no matter how upset I might have been, I'm sure I would have forgiven them for keeping it secret.

I had spent much of the past year trying to tamp down the simmering anger I felt toward my adoptive parents. After all, it wasn't as if there hadn't been opportunities to tell me the truth. My longtime friend Frank, a fellow adoptee, reminded me of that during one of our many phone conversations.

"Trish, I know you asked your dad all the right questions. He had the answers all along but wouldn't tell you. What a waste of your energy... for your whole life, really."

"Wow, you're right," I said. "He had the answers all along."

Rather than focusing on my anger, though, I had tried to focus on finding out as much as I could about my birth parents and the family that shared my genetics. The positive feelings that came from their unconditional acceptance and willingness to help me on my journey were so welcome and healing that I was reluctant to examine my resentment toward my adoptive parents. I set it aside, to be dealt with later.

Eventually I tried to look at the situation from a different perspective. My son Jesse had told me early on that he never felt the "humming in his DNA" when he was around my relatives—only when he was around his father's (my ex-husband's) family. I didn't understand exactly what he meant until I met my birth mother's family and later, my birth father's family.

If there was really something to Jesse's theory that the electrical impulses in our cells can recognize and respond to the electrical impulses in the cells of those we're related to when we're in their presence, then it was possible Bernadette and Wayne felt the same lack of connection to me as I did around them.

Bernadette had tried so hard to turn me into the daughter she wanted. She didn't understand that I was biologically incapable of being that daughter—not just because of my larger body and distinct nose but because it was in my DNA to love poetry and dance, to laugh too loud and act too boisterous, and to "waste time" pondering the meaning of the Tree of Life. Bernadette's biological makeup might have been crying out to connect to a girl who wanted to sit up straight and play the piano. Someone who would never need to be told to "settle down now." A girl who was more conventional, who would activate the humming in Bernadette's own DNA. It must have been hard on her. After a more than a year of being angry with her, I was starting to feel empathy for her.

I had been fortunate to be able to get answers to so many of my questions. I was also beginning to understand that there were some "why's" that would remain a mystery. Acceptance would take time, but it was slowly making its presence known.

A balmy summer in Seattle was transitioning into autumn on the day I met Uncle Sean for dinner. I arrived at the restaurant a little early and was chatting with the two friendly women at the next table when Sean arrived. I noticed how his energy immediately filled up the room, not to mention his large physical presence. I was looking forward to our first one-on-one visit.

Over our steak dinners we talked about many different subjects. He had brought his Bible and we discussed how God looks after orphans and widows in their distress. I assured him that I knew God had been looking after me my entire life.

We talked about the Tree of Life and once again, I was excited to have found someone who shared my passion about the imagery and meaning of the tree in our lives—how it represents physical and spiritual nourishment and is a symbol of growth and resurrection.

As we were getting ready to leave the restaurant, I pointed out that we had talked very little about my mother, Patsy. Sean replied that she was a person who lived very much in the present moment and not in the past.

On my drive home, I glanced at the clock and noted it said 9:19 p.m. The date was 9/19/19. Strange. Then the clock clicked over to 9:20. I took it as a sign that I could not remain frozen in time and must move forward.

CHAPTER TWENTY-ONE

The family newsletter made it official. The fact that I was adopted was now known by all my adoptive father's family members, if they hadn't known it before.

"As we continue to research and uncover new information about our family heritage, we are finding a high proportion of adopting and fostering children in need that has taken place in each generation.

"Most of the children are aware of their beginnings but some are not. In these days of increased transparency, much of what was hidden in the past is being discovered through DNA testing."

The "ripple effect" of my adoption story, which had touched my birth father Tom's family and my childhood friends and neighbors, had also affected my father Wayne's family. One relative told me they were all talking more about what the word "family" really meant.

I still considered my parents' relatives to be part of my family.

"You don't get to 'un-cousin' me," I told Kevin, who had sent last year's shocking letter to me.

"Don't worry, I won't," he assured me with a chuckle.

I knew the relationships that I'd built over nearly six decades were not likely to change, and if I did decide to attend another family reunion in eastern Oregon, at least this time I would know the truth. The history I had been taught about Norma the schoolteacher, Michael the German stowaway, and the rest of my father's ancestors was not my true history—and I was okay with that. I had learned how to separate the issue of family from the issue of personal family history.

At the beginning of my search, I was so excited to meet my birth parents' family, the people who set my DNA to "humming." The foundation upon which I had built my life—my identity as Wayne and Bernadette's biological daughter—no longer existed. It was tempting to replace that foundation with a new identity as Patsy and Tom's daughter, especially since I had been lovingly welcomed by their family members. With help from a counselor, though, I realized that my foundation, my identity, could not be built out of my relationship with other people, no matter who they were. I had to find that wholeness within myself.

My journey had helped me own the parts of myself that were not readily accepted in my adoptive family but were honored in my birth family. That validation was a missing piece of the puzzle I needed to solve.

I also came to recognize that the insecurity of my childhood had created a dynamic where I over-attached to people. When my parents could not fulfill my emotional needs, I turned to my neighborhood. When the kids I grew up with dispersed around the country, I was the one who organized the reunions, the one who kept us all in touch. And that was the pattern that followed me through life.

It was as if God turned a light on in my brain and I

could finally see the truth, not only about my parentage but about myself.

Every "ripple effect" of my story wasn't necessarily positive. How do you explain to your children that what they believed to be true about their family history was false? My kids all had to process the shocking revelation along with me, in their own ways.

My son Jesse admitted that "It resolved some questions that had bothered me a little over the years." Still, it was a challenge for all of them to be forced to mentally reframe a lifetime of memories.

I wished I could have made it easier for them.

CHAPTER TWENTY-TWO

As fall wore on, I began making holiday plans. Over the past sixteen months I had met dozens of new relatives, but one group I hadn't spent much time with yet was the "southern California" wing of my birth father's family. I owned a timeshare unit in San Diego, so I made arrangements to spend Christmas in sunny California.

I arrived at the San Diego airport a few days before Christmas to find I hadn't escaped the Pacific Northwest rain after all. My second cousin Desmond—whose mother had been close to my birth mother Patsy—was waiting to greet me, along with his significant other, Mary.

"Sorry, we were hoping it would be a sunny day. Mary made lunch reservations at a restaurant by the water, but we might have to eat inside."

"Oh, that's no problem," I said. "I'm just so excited to finally meet you in person. After all, you were the first person I spoke to who actually knew my mother and you were the one who pointed me in the direction of her brothers. Without you, I'm not sure what I would have done."

We chatted at lunch as if we were old friends. He shared more of his stories about our ancestor, my great-grandfather Joe Higgins, who had owned a candy store in Canada. We talked about the importance of family history, and Mary said she was now planning to write down some stories about her own family for her children. Another "ripple effect."

Desmond and Mary dropped me off at my timeshare and I settled in for a short break. My son wasn't due to arrive until the next day, but I had another visit on my schedule. Yet another cousin!

By the time my cousin Bernie picked me up, the rain had turned into a torrential downpour. So much for a sunny holiday in San Diego. We headed to his sister Maureen's house. The first thing Maureen said when she saw me was, "Oh my god, Bernie, she looks just like our mother!" It was the second time I had been told how much I looked like my father's sister Virginia.

"I was just seeing Uncle Tom in her," Bernie volunteered. I wondered what they would think if I confessed that several times in the past few months, I had looked in the mirror and seen flashes of my birth parents in my reflection. I decided they might think I was crazy, so I kept it to myself.

I mentioned to Bernie that I had been struck by the intense kindness of my birth father's family members. "Even the ones who don't know each other seem to have this same trait."

"I think it's our family's strength," he said. "Some people see kindness as a sign of weakness, but that's not the case with us. I think it's a quality all our parents shared and then passed down to their children. Kindness is expected."

I had started the day in Seattle, flown more than a thousand miles, and visited with two of my relatives, so by the time I unlocked the front door to my timeshare that night I was exhausted. The next day I would see some familiar faces, including Mike, the second cousin who had first contacted me after taking a DNA test, his mother, Kit, and Bernie, the cousin I had just met.

The Christmas Eve gathering was held at Mike's brother's hillside home, which had been elegantly decorated for the season. "There's a lovely view from the deck," I was told, so I joined Kit and a few others in admiring the vista and sharing stories about my birth father Tom as well as Kit's late husband, the pilot who had been so influenced by Tom as a youngster. I had brought copies of some of the Mahoney family home movies with me from Seattle, and I could hear them playing in the background as the California relatives enjoyed watching the antics of their Pacific Northwest relatives.

The meal had a distinctive southwestern twist, courtesy of Cousin Bernie. The children sang Christmas songs and put on a show. A surprise pregnancy was announced. Pictures were taken and once again I found myself being scrutinized in the best of ways. My eye color was similar to a certain cousin's. My face reminded someone else of another relative. The goodwill toward me was palpable. My DNA was humming for sure.

All too soon it was time to leave, and plans were made to meet for a final lunch the day after Christmas.

Jesse and his wife Cortney understandably wanted to spend some time exploring San Diego while they had the chance. I told them to enjoy themselves and said I was a bit tired anyway.

After a couple of whirlwind days, I found myself alone on Christmas Day.

CHAPTER TWENTY-THREE

I recognized the irony in the fact that despite having gained dozens of new family members, I was spending Christmas by myself in my timeshare unit. On the one hand, I welcomed the chance to rest; on the other hand, it brought to mind painful thoughts about the Christmases I had never been able to have—and never would have—with my birth parents.

I gave myself permission to grieve.

For almost a year and a half, I had been on a rollercoaster ride. The highs were the times I felt my DNA humming and the times I had a breakthrough about myself and my life. The lows were the times I was overcome by grief over what I'd lost and anger that I had been lied to for so long.

As I rested in my timeshare, I reflected on what I had learned in my journey, and it came down to this. When it comes to family, there are three elements to consider: the constructs of a family; the presence of love or dysfunction; and the value of a biochemical connection (the "humming in your DNA").

Children cannot choose the family they grow up with. Obviously, most are raised by their biological parents and they set out on the journey of life with their biological siblings. Other children are chosen by strangers who want to provide a home and—one hopes—love.

If the family of our childhood is inadequate, we search for another construct that will serve our needs. As a child, I tried to create a family out of my neighbors. In adulthood, some of them remained close enough to be considered "family" along with my children.

The presence of love is key. There are many ways to show love. My father Wayne might have felt he showed his love by going to work every day and providing for the family, including me. Maybe he didn't feel that any other expression of love was necessary. My mother Bernadette was not someone who was given to gushing about anything, let alone how she felt about me. But she took me into her home when she didn't have to, which is an act of love.

There is something else beyond words that can show love: Let the child be her (or his) authentic self. Every flower needs a different environment to grow, and if a flower isn't growing, you need to change the environment.

Tolerance for differences and kindness are especially important for an adopted child.

Sometimes the dysfunction in the family doesn't leave any room for love to grow. To most outsiders my family looked perfectly fine, but in truth there was dysfunction, which interfered with being able to feel (or show) love.

When I felt the "humming in my DNA," it changed everything for me. Being with the people I was biologically connected to was healing. Did that mean adopted children who never meet their birth families cannot be truly happy? Certainly, my relative Kit was one example of an adoptee who didn't need the third element to feel complete, like I did.

In today's world there is no need to keep the truth from adopted children. No one should have to grow up "believing you're crazy because you couldn't figure out the family dynamics and only knew something just didn't add up"—as my friend Frank said to me during one of our conversations. Finding out the truth that I was adopted relieved me of all the confusion around family dynamics that I had carried around for so long.

I was buried in these deep thoughts when a friend called from home. Whatever loneliness and grief I was feeling disappeared as we spent the next two hours talking. She chased my Christmas blues away.

The next day I met everyone for lunch at a Mexican restaurant in San Diego's Old Town. The wonderful food, laughter, and general good cheer was a perfect way to end the holiday visit.

It felt as if the rollercoaster ride I had been on was finally gliding toward the "Exit" sign. By this time I had met virtually every member of my birth parents' families and each person had helped me go a bit farther on my journey. I hugged everyone and we exchanged mutual promises to keep in touch.

Jesse and Cortney headed back to Colorado and I boarded my plane for Seattle. As we soared through the sky, I looked out the window and thanked God for the way my story had turned out. It seemed impossible that only eighteen months ago I had torn open an envelope and stared at a piece of paper that listed my name as... blank.

I am no longer "blank." I am Patricia Havens, and I have filled in all the blanks of my life.

AFTERWORD

It has now been two-and-a-half years since I learned I was adopted, and I continue to be grateful for the way the members of my birth parents' families have welcomed me as one of their own. As I was writing the final chapters of this book, a postcard arrived from the cousin who had shared his childhood memories of "hanging out" with my birth father Tom in Seattle. His recollections came early in my journey and gave me an insight into my father that I never would have had otherwise.

Hi Patricia,

I want you to know that I truly appreciate all the effort you have made to reach out to me over the past couple of years. It's been a pleasant gift to get to know you and hear your story.

In particular, I felt grateful to have the knowledge of your life and the legacy Tom left. As you know, he was my favorite uncle. Having talked and corresponded with you, I know my favorite parts of him live on. His kindness, his love of a good story, his sense of humor, his enjoyment of connecting with others. They are alive today in you. It is a joy to know this.

Sincerely, Tim

Along with everyone else, at this time I am experiencing life during a pandemic that has caused too many families to lose their loved ones. It has reinforced what I have learned over the past few years—the importance of family, whatever form that takes.

I wish all people the sense of belonging that we all yearn for.

ACKNOWLEDGMENTS

I could not have written this book without the help of all the family members who generously shared their memories, family lore, historical documents, and so much more with me. Thank you to the Mahoney, Higgins, Eberhardt, Geiger, Mallory, Casey, and McNeilly families. I am thankful I was able to grow up surrounded by so many caring people who I still consider to be family.

I am fortunate to have a wonderful group of friends who have stuck with me through the ups and downs of life for five decades, and they supported this project in many ways. Special thanks to Celia, Gayle, Dawn, Gretchen, and Cherie.

Through a stroke of serendipity, I crossed paths with Stephanie McMullen, who organized and edited my stories for this book.

Most importantly, I want to thank my parents for giving me a home and my birth parents for giving me a chance to experience life.

APPENDIX - FAMILY RECIPES

One of the meaningful ways I was welcomed into my birth parents' families was through the sharing of family recipes. Here are a few that I particularly enjoyed.

Bernie's Easy Chicken Enchiladas Verde

Ingredients:

1 lb. cooked boneless skinless chicken (diced or shredded)
1-1/2 lbs. shredded blend of Monterey jack and cheddar cheese
1 28-oz. can green chile enchilada sauce
2 10-oz. cans diced tomatoes with green chiles (drain off liquid)
1/2 c. diced green onions or scallions
1/2 c. sliced olives
10 flour tortillas (8" size)

Preparation: Preheat oven to 350 degrees. Mix chicken, 1/3 cheese, both cans of tomatoes and chiles, and 1 cup of green enchilada sauce in a large bowl. Pour 1 cup green enchilada sauce into 9x13x2 Pyrex baking dish. Spread sauce evenly on bottom of dish. Fill tortillas with chicken/cheese/tomato/chile mixture and roll to form enchiladas. Arrange seam side down in baking dish. Pour remaining sauce over enchiladas. Spread remaining cheese over enchiladas and cover with aluminum foil. Bake for 30 minutes. Remove foil, sprinkle onions and olives over enchiladas. Continue baking 10 minutes or until cheese starts turning brown. Let cool for 5 minutes and serve with salsa, sour cream, and/or guacamole.

Patsy's Shortbread

Ingredients:

1 c. sugar
1 c. Crisco
4 c. flour
1 c. butter
1/2 t. salt

Preparation:

Mix together and bake at 300 degrees for one hour.

Patsy's Date Nut Bread

Ingredients:

3 c. flour
4 tsp. baking powder
1/2 c. sugar
1-1/2 tsp. salt
3/4 c. dates
1/2 c. nuts
1 egg (beaten)
1-1/2 c. milk
2 T. shortening

Preparation:

Bake at 350 degrees for 1-1/4 hours.

Kit's Au Gratin Potatoes

Ingredients:

5 lbs. russet potatoes
2 c. milk
1/2 c. half-and-half cream
1 small can green chiles
1 small can jalapeños (medium temp.)
3 T. melted butter
1/2 c. shredded Parmesan cheese
12 oz. pkg. shredded pepper jack cheese
12 oz. pkg. shredded cheddar cheese
Salt and pepper to taste

Preparation:

Butter a 9x13 baking dish. Mix cheese, chiles, milk in bowl. Pour mixture over potatoes and bake for 45 minutes at 350 degrees.

Mary's Johnny Marzetti Casserole

Ingredients:

2 T. margarine
2 large onions
1/2 lb. mushrooms
1/2 c. celery
1/2 c. green pepper
1 tsp. minced garlic
1 lb. hamburger
1 15-oz. can tomato sauce
1 tsp. salt
1 tsp. pepper
8 oz. elbow macaroni
8 oz. shredded cheddar cheese

Preparation:

Cook vegetables first in margarine until onions are done. Add meat until done (pinkish). Add tomato sauce. Stir in macaroni and cheese. Mix all together and bake at 350 degrees for 30 minutes.

Made in the USA
Columbia, SC
09 November 2024